Herbert Puchta & Jeff Stranks

English in Mind

Second edition

Student's Book 1

CAMBRIDGE
UNIVERSITY PRESS

Speaking & Functions	Listening	Reading	Writing
Talking about school Talking about hobbies Expressing likes and dislikes	An interview about a hobby	Article: An unusual hobby Culture in mind: School clubs	Email about your hobbies and interests
Talking about housework Last but not least: arranging to meet and making plans	Radio interview with a volunteer in Namibia	Article: Helping at a hospital Photostory: Let's give him a hand	Email about organising a party
Talking about the past Talking about when/where people were born	Presentation of 'my hero'	Article: Erin Brockovich Culture in mind: Remembering heroes	Three paragraphs about your hero
Asking about the past Retelling a story Last but not least: Alibi – a game	Television story Song: *You've Got A Friend In Me*	Article: The ping pong friendship that changed the world Photostory: Not a nice thing to say	Diary entry or email about an enjoyable weekend
Talking about obligations Describing job requirements Talking about people and their jobs	Talking about success Descriptions of future jobs	Article: What does 'success' mean? Article: Following a dream Culture in mind: Teenagers: earning money	Description of a job
Talking about food and fitness Last but not least: talking about food and places to eat	School canteen dialogue	Article: A long and healthy life Photostory: A double ice cream …	Paragraph about food and fitness
Comparing things Talking about learning English	Interviews about language learning An interview with David Crystal	Article: Speaking in many tongues Culture in mind: Teen talk	Description or email about language learning
Talking about arrangements Discussing holiday plans Last but not least: information gap: talking about holidays	Radio show about family holidays Dialogue about holiday plans	Magazine article: Family holidays can be fun! Travel brochure: Welcome to Cape Town – the city that has everything! Photostory: Having fun?	Email about a trip
Making predictions Talking about your future life Talking about fortune telling	Future predictions Song: *When I'm Sixty-four*	Article: Getting the future wrong! Culture in mind: Fortune telling	Text predicting the future
Describing actions Relating Hermann Maier's life story Describing the weather Last but not least: information gap about famous sportspeople	A weather forecast Dialogue about the life of Hermann Maier	Article: Jungle survival Photostory: Keep on running	Email giving advice to a friend
Talking about intentions Talking about a song	Dialogue about a New Year's Eve party Song: *Wonderful World, Beautiful People*	Article: In New York for New Year's Eve Culture in mind: Reggae Music	Email about New Year's Eve
Expressing future possibilities Discussing bravery Last but not least: talking about situations where you were brave / not brave	Dialogues about bravery	Article: Subway hero Photostory: Chicken	Description of a film, book or TV programme
Giving advice and recommendations Talking about what somebody is like	Dialogue about different customs around the world A quiz about UK culture	Quiz: What do you know about UK culture? Culture in mind: Heroic Ulises on a journey of hope	Email giving tips to a tourist
Talking about life experiences Last but not least: talking about things you've never done	Conversation about strange world records	Article: You've never seen anything like this! Article: He holds the record – for records! Photostory: What's the next thing?	Email about a visit to Los Angeles

Welcome section

A PEOPLE

1 Greetings and introductions

a ▶ CD1 T1 Complete the dialogue with the words in the box. Then listen and check.

~~fine~~ ~~I'm~~ ~~name's~~ ~~Nice~~ ~~this~~ ~~you~~

Liz: Hi. My [1] *name's* Liz.

Monica: Hello, Liz. [2] **I'm** Monica.

Liz: Nice to meet you. Excuse me a moment. Hi, Jack. How are you?

Jack: I'm [3] **fine** , thanks. How about [4] **you** ?

Liz: I'm OK, thanks. Monica, [5] **this** is my friend, Jack.

Monica: [6] **Nice** to meet you, Jack.

Jack: Nice to meet you too, Monica.

b Work in a group of three. Have conversations like the one in Exercise 1a.

2 The verb *be*

a Look at the pictures. Fill in the spaces with the correct form of *be* (positive or negative).

b ▶ CD1 T2 Complete the dialogue with the correct form of the verb *be*. Then listen and check.

Jack: Hi. My name [1] **i's** Jack, and this [2] **is** Monica. She [3] **is** from Italy.

Marek: Nice to meet you. I [4] ~~from~~ **am** Marek, and those two people [5] **are** my friends, Barbara and Adam. [6] **are** you from Rome, Monica?

Monica: No, I [7] **am** from Milan. Where [8] **are** you from?

Marek: We [9] **are** from Poland. Adam and I [10] **am** from Warsaw and Barbara [11] **is** from Gdansk. [12] **are** you on holiday in Cambridge?

Monica: No, I [13] **am** not. I'm a student at a language school here. [14] **are** you all students?

Marek: Yes, we [15] **are** . We [16] **are** at a language school too.

LOOK!

My name's ... (I → my)
What's your name? (you → your)

1 They **'re** from China.

2 I **am** from the USA.

3 I **am** American, I ~~from~~ **not** Brazilian!

4 She **is** British.

5 He **is not** British, he **is** from Turkey!

6 We **not** from China, we **are** Japanese.

c Work with a partner. Ask and answer questions about the people in Exercise 2b.

A: *Is Monica from Poland?*

B: *No, she isn't. She's from Milan, in Italy. Are Marek and Adam ... ?*

3 Possessive adjectives

Read Liz's email from her new e-pal, Laura. Fill in the spaces with *my, your, his, her, our* or *their*.

Hey Liz,

Thanks for [1] *your* last email! And I loved the photos of [2] _your'_ friends and family – I looked at them yesterday. [3] _your_ mum and dad look really nice in the photo. So now I'll tell you about me and [4] _my_ family here in Switzerland.

I've got two brothers. [5] _their_ names are Lukas and Andreas and they're 16 and 19. My mother is American and [6] _her_ name is Christine. Dad is Swiss German – he's from Zürich, and [7] _His_ name is Dieter. We live in Geneva. [8] _my_ house has got four bedrooms and a small garden. We've got a dog and we think he's lovely. [9] _His_ name's Zak.

Please tell me some more about [10] _your_ friends. I'd really like to meet more English people!

See ya,

Laura

4 have/has got

a ▶ CD1 T3 Listen to the dialogue between Marek and Monica and answer the questions.

1 How many brothers and sisters has Marek got? _he have got a brother._
2 How many brothers and sisters has Monica got? _she have got a two sisters_

b ▶ CD1 T3 Listen again and complete the table.

	Age	Colour of hair	Colour of eyes
Milos	19	*fair*	green
Silvia	12	black	brown
Lisa	9	black	blue

c Follow the lines and make sentences with *have/has got*.

My brother hasn't got a computer.

1 My brother	2 My parents	3 My aunt and uncle

4 My friend's brother	5 Sid's father	6 My grandfather

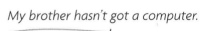

1 Colours

a Write the colours.

1 _white_   2 _block_ ✓   3 _brown_ ✓   4 _pink_ ✓   5 _grey_ ✓

6 _red_ ✓   7 _green_ ✓   8 _yelow_ ✓   9 _blue_ ✓   10 _orange_ ✓

b Work in a small group. Find something in your classroom for each colour.

The floor's grey.   The desks are brown.   The wall is yellow.

2 Rooms and furniture

a Look at the pictures. Write the names of the rooms (A–F).

b Look at the pictures. Label the furniture. Use the words in the box.

> armchair bath bed chair cooker cupboard door
> fridge shower sink sofa table toilet window

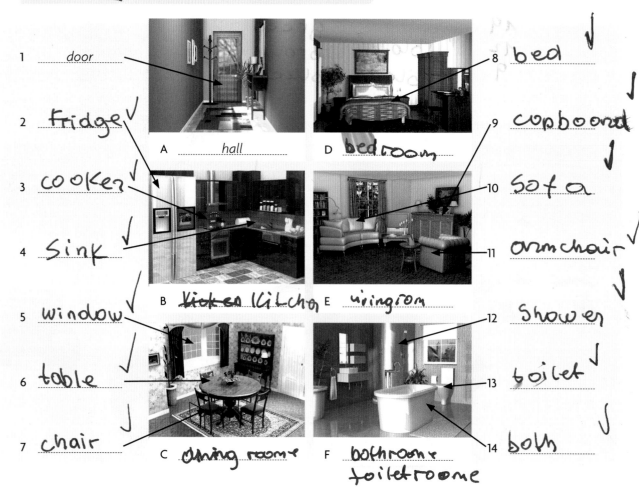

1 _door_

2 _fridge_ ✓

3 _cooker_ ✓

4 _sink_ ✓

5 _window_ ✓

6 _table_ ✓

7 _chair_ ✓

A _hall_

B _Kitchen_

C _dining room_

D _bedroom_

E _livingrom_

F _bathroom toiletroome_

8 _bed_ ✓

9 _cupboard_ ✓

10 _sofa_ ✓

11 _armchair_ ✓

12 _shower_ ✓

13 _toilet_ ✓

14 _bath_ ✓

3 There is / There are

a Complete the sentences. Use *There's a/an* or *There are*.

1   *There's a* black table in the dining room.
2   *There are* two doors in our living room.
3   *there are* four white chairs in our kitchen.
4   *there are* three posters on the wall in my bedroom.
5   *There's a* red sofa in my sister's room.

b Play a memory game. Look at the picture for 30 seconds. Then make sentences with *There's* or *There are*.

There are two windows.

4 Prepositions of place

a Look at the picture again and say where things are. Use the prepositions in the box.

in   on   under   next to   behind   between

b Draw a plan of your house/flat. Talk about it to your partner.

There's a hall, a kitchen, …
There are three bedrooms. There's a bathroom next to my parents' bedroom.
In the living room there's a green sofa and there are two brown armchairs. The television is between …

C ACTIVITIES

1 Activity verbs

Match the verbs with the pictures.

open   close   run   swim   listen   read   jump   ~~laugh~~   cry   write   shout   smile

1 *laugh*

2 _____

3 _____

4 _____

5 _____

6 _____

7 _____

8 _____

9 _____

10 _____

11 _____

12 _____

2 Imperatives

Write what the people are saying. Use the verbs from Exercise 1 above.

1 *Don't laugh!*

3 Adverbs of frequency

a Put the adverbs in the correct places in the diagram.

hardly ever   sometimes   always   usually

100%						0%

1 _____ 2 _____ 3 *often* 4 _____ 5 _____ 6 *never*

LOOK!

We put the adverb of frequency:
– **after** the verb *be*, e.g. *I'm always late*
– **before** other verbs, e.g. *We always go to the cinema on Friday.*

b Write sentences that are true for you. Complete the sentences with *always, usually, often, sometimes, hardly ever* or *never*.

1 I _____ play football after school.

2 My teachers _____ give us homework on Friday afternoons.

3 I _____ go to the cinema at the weekend.

4 My best friend _____ comes to my house at the weekend.

5 I _____ watch TV in the morning.

c Work with a partner. Tell him/her about your sentences in Exercise 3b.

A: *I sometimes play football after school.*

B: *Really? I never play football after school, but I sometimes play at the weekend.*

4 Object pronouns

Put the object pronouns in the sentences.

you   us   ~~them~~   me   him   her

1 My mother really likes eggs but I hate _____them_____ .

2 Sara's my best friend. She phones _____ every day.

3 My brother's got a poster of Shakira. He really likes _____ !

4 Peter is really nice. I really like _____ .

5 Have you got a problem with your homework? I can help _____ .

6 My sister and I like our uncle. He gives _____ great birthday presents.

5 can/can't for ability

a ▶ CD1 T4   Listen to Marek and Liz talking about what they can and can't do. Fill in the first two columns in the table.

✓ ✓ = Yes.   ✓ = Yes, but not very well.
✗ = No.

	Marek	Liz	You	Your partner
1	✗			
2				
3				
4				

b Write sentences. Use the information in the table.

Marek can't swim. Liz can swim, but not very well.

c What about you? Fill in the *You* column in the table.

d Work with a partner. Ask questions and fill in the *Your partner* column in the table.

A: *Can you swim?*

B: *Yes, I can. Can you ... ?*

D IN TOWN AND SHOPPING

1 Places

Look at the pictures. Where can you see or buy these things? Write 1–8 in the boxes.

> 1 café   2 disco   3 ~~cinema~~   4 shoe shop   5 bookshop   6 station   7 clothes shop   8 post office

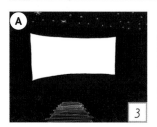
A
3

B

C

D

E

F

G

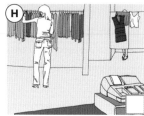
H

2 *There is/are* (negative and questions) + *a/an/any*

a Match the beginnings and endings.

1 Are there   a   a good disco in town.
2 Is there   b   a post office here?
3 There aren't   c   any good films at the cinema?
4 There's   d   any people in the bookshop.

b Complete the questions and short answers.

1 *Are there* any discos here?
   (✗) No, there *aren't* .
2 _____ a station in your town?
   (✓) Yes, there _____ .
3 _____ a post office in this street?
   (✓) Yes, _____ .
4 _____ any nice clothes in the shop?
   (✗) No, _____ .

c Complete the sentences with *a* or *any*.

1 There aren't *any* good clothes shops here.
2 Is there _____ post office near here?
3 There's _____ good shoe shop in this street.
4 Are there _____ discos in this town?

d What can you say about the place where you live? Use the places in Exercise 1 and the questions and sentences in Exercises 2b and 2c to help you.

3 Times

Write the sentences.

1 *The Post Office opens at eight thirty and closes at five thirty.*

Café 9.15–21.00

DISCO 22.00–01.30

2 _____
3 _____

4 _____

Next film: 19.45–21.30

Bookshop 10.00–18.00 (Saturdays 10.00–12.15)

5 _____
6 _____

4 Clothes

a Write the letters in the correct order to make words. Write them under the pictures.

> sreds skrit hirst scosk hoses muprej ~~siThrt~~ najse scraf inatrers usrtosre tekcaj

1
$24.00

T-shirt

2 €118.00

3 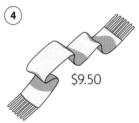 £120.00

4  $9.50

5 £5.25

6  €56.50

7 £195.00

8 €54.75

9  $47.00

10  £85.00

11 $62.99

12 €39.99

b Say what colour the clothes are.

The T-shirt's blue.   _The trainers are black._

c Work with a partner. Ask and answer.

A: _What colour is your favourite shirt?_
B: _Blue. What colour are your favourite shoes?_
A: _They're ..._

5 Money and prices

a Draw a line to match the words and symbols.

1 £   2 €   3 $
dollar   euro   pound

b ▶ CD1 T5 Work with a partner. Say the prices. Then listen and check your answers.

1 £12.00   4 $11.25
2 €25.00   5 €17.50
3 $125   6 £15.99

> ## LOOK!
>
> - We write £12.00 – we say _twelve pounds._
> - We write €7.25 – we say _seven euros twenty-five._
> - We write £5.99 – we say _five pounds ninety-nine._
> - We write $125.00 – we say _a hundred and twenty-five dollars._

c Work with a partner. Say the prices of the clothes in Exercise 4a.

The T-shirt is twenty-four dollars.
The trainers are a hundred and twenty pounds.

d Work with a partner. Ask and answer.

A: _How much is the T-shirt?_
B: _It's twenty-four dollars. How much are the trainers?_

1 Free time

* Present simple (positive and negative; questions and short answers)
* *like + -ing*
* Vocabulary: hobbies and interests, school subjects

1 Read and listen

a Look at the pictures. How old do you think the girl is? What is her hobby? Read the text quickly to check your ideas.

b ▶ CD1 T6 Now read the text again and listen. Answer the questions.

1 Where is Claire from?
2 How is Claire different from her friends?
3 Why don't Hannah and Kate go near the hives?
4 What does Claire like doing on Sunday afternoon?
5 Why does she keep the money from the honey she sells?

An unusual hobby

Claire Williams is 15. She's from Wales. Her friends play volleyball and go to the cinema. They like swimming and dancing. But Claire doesn't. She has an unusual hobby: beekeeping. She's got four beehives. She isn't sure, but she thinks she's got about 40,000 bees.

In the spring, this is a typical Sunday for Claire:

7.30 Claire gets up. She has breakfast with her parents.

8.30 Claire puts on her special clothes and goes out into the garden. She feeds the bees with sugar and water. She sometimes takes photos of the bees, too.

11.00 Claire's friends Hannah and Kate come round. They don't go near the hives. 'We enjoy watching Claire with the bees,' they say. 'But we're a bit scared of them!' Claire talks to her friends for a while. Then Hannah and Kate say goodbye, and Claire goes back to the bees.

1.15 It's lunchtime. Claire likes telling her family about bees. 'They fly 80,000 kilometres to make one kilo of honey!' she says. 'And they visit about three million flowers!'

3.00 In the afternoon, Claire stays in her room. She loves reading about bees on the internet or in books.

In the summer, Claire's bees produce about 40 kilos of honey. Claire takes the honey to a little shop and sells it. She doesn't spend the money, because she wants to buy more beehives!

2 Grammar

✱ Present simple (positive and negative)

a Look at the examples. Then complete the rule.

*They **play** volleyball.*
*Claire **gets** up at 7.30.*
*Claire's friends **come** round.*
*She **takes** the honey to a little shop.*

> **RULE:** We use the present simple for things which happen regularly or which are always true.
>
> With *I*, _____, *we* and _____ we use the base form of the verb. With *he*, *she* and *it* we add _____ .

🔍 LOOK!

With *he*, *she* and *it*, some verbs end in *es*.

-sh   they wash – she wash**es**
-ch   we teach – he teach**es**,
        I go – she go**es**

If the verb ends with consonant + *y*, the ending is *ies*.

they fly – it fl**ies**
you study – he stud**ies**

b Complete the sentences. Use the present simple form of the verbs.

1 Sara ___loves___ (love) films.
2 My friends **hates** (hate) sport.
3 You **take** (take) good photographs.
4 Mrs Jameson **teaching** (teach) us English.
5 My father **flying** (fly) to France twice a year.
6 My mum **ready** (read) a lot of books.
7 We **going** (go) to school at 8.30 in the morning.

c Look at the pictures. Write present simple sentences. Use *like*, *love* or *hate* and a word from the box.

cats football ~~apples~~ ice cream bananas winter

1 He *likes apples.* _____

2 I **see like banana**

3 She **like icream** .

4 They **like sit** .

5 She **like winter** .

6 We **lik foodbol**.

d Look at the examples and complete the table.

*Claire **doesn't spend** the money.*
*They **don't go** near the hives.*

Positive	Negative
I/you/we/they **run**	I/you/we/they _____ (**do not**) run
he/she/it **runs**	he/she/it _____ (**does not**) run

e Complete the sentences. Use the present simple form of the verbs.

1 I ___don't like___ (not like) this kind of music.
2 We **Don't eat** (not eat) a lot of meat at home.
3 My parents **speak** (speak) French.
4 I **Don't know** (not know) his phone number.
5 My brother **gets up** (get up) late at the weekend.
6 My father **doesn't drive** (not drive) to work.

f Make the sentences negative.

1 My brother spends lots of money on clothes.

My brother doesn't spend lots of money on clothes.

2 I get up early on Sunday.

i don't get up early on sunday

3 My sister watches a lot of TV.

My sister don't watches a lot of TV

4 I buy my CDs in that shop.

I didn't buy my CDs in that shop

5 You know the answer.

You don't know the answer

3 Vocabulary

✱ Hobbies and interests

a ▶ CD1 T7 Match the activities with the pictures. Write 1–9 in the boxes. Then listen, check and repeat.

1 going to the cinema
2 reading
3 swimming
4 painting
5 playing computer games
6 dancing
7 listening to music
8 playing the guitar
9 running

b Match words from the three lists to make five true sentences.

	play	magazines.
	plays	the guitar.
	don't play	pop music.
	doesn't play	computer games.
I	listen to	tennis.
My friends	doesn't listen to	to football matches.
My brother	go	a newspaper every day.
My sister	goes	
	doesn't go	
	read	
	don't read	
	doesn't read	

Vocabulary bank Turn to page 112.

4 Grammar

★ *like + -ing*

a Look at the examples and complete the rule.

*They like **swimming** and **dancing**.*
*We enjoy **watching** Claire with the bees.*
*She loves **reading** about bees.*
*I hate **getting** up early!*

> **RULE:** We often use the .... form after verbs of liking and not liking, for example, *like, don't like, love* and *hate*.

LOOK!

If the verb ends in *e*, we drop the *e* before *-ing*.
dance – danc**ing**, smile – smil**ing**

If a short verb ends in vowel + consonant, we double the last letter before *-ing*.
swim – swi**mm**ing, run – ru**nn**ing

b Complete the sentences. Use the *-ing* form of the verbs in the box.

> ride   run   play   go   ~~listen~~   talk

1 Maria hates __listening__ to jazz.
2 My brother doesn't like .... games.
3 My sister loves .... her bike.
4 My dad enjoys .... on the beach.
5 I love .... to my friends on the phone.
6 We love .... to football matches at the weekend.

5 Speak

a Work with a partner. Talk about the hobbies in Exercise 3.

I love ...   I (don't) like/enjoy ...
I hate ...   I'm (not) good at ...

b Make notes and tell other people in your class about your partner's hobbies.

6 Listen

a ▶ CD1 T8 Listen to the interview. Which picture shows Mark's hobby?

① ② ③

b ▶ CD1 T8 Listen again. Write *T* (true) or *F* (false).

1 Mark gives shows once a month. ☐
2 He learns new tricks on the internet. ☐
3 Mark practises every day. ☐
4 Mark's brother wants to be a magician. ☐

7 Pronunciation

▶ CD1 T9 and T10 Turn to page 110.

8 Grammar

★ Present simple (questions and short answers)

a Read the examples about Mark's hobby and complete the table.

***Do** your friends **know** about your hobby? Yes, they **do**.*
***Does** it **take** a long time to learn? Yes, it **does**.*
***Do** you **tell** your brother how to do the tricks?*
*No, I **don't**.*

Questions	Short answers
.... I/you/we/they study English?	Yes, I/you/we/they **do**. No, I/you/we/they .... (**do not**).
.... he/she/it like study English?	Yes, he/she/it .... No, he/she/it **doesn't** (............ **not**).

b Complete the questions and short answers.

1 A: __Does__ Jeremy like swimming?
   B: __Yes, he does__ .... (✓) .

2 A: .... you study French?
   B: .... (✗) .

3 A: .... your friends listen to music?
   B: .... (✓) .

4 A: .... she go to your school?
   B: .... (✓) .

Culture in mind

9 Read and listen

a Nadia, Sarah and Caroline go to the same school. Read the text quickly and find:

1 five subjects that they study during the day

2 three different clubs at the school

b Look at the pictures. Which things are school subjects? Which are clubs? Write *S* (subject) or *C* (club) in the boxes.

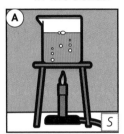
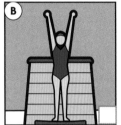

A   S

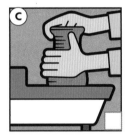

C   D

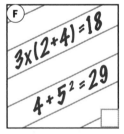

E   English Dictionary   F $3 \times (2+4) = 18$ $4 + 5^2 = 29$

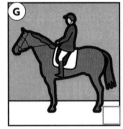

G   H   Noms Français

I   J

School clubs

Caroline, Sarah and Nadia are all students at Park School, in the north-west of England. It's an all-girls school – the Park School for boys is not far away in the same town.

The three girls are all 14 and they're in year 9. During the school day, they study subjects on the National Curriculum: subjects like English, Maths, History, Geography, PE and ICT (Information and Communication Technology). They also study two or three languages (for example, French or Spanish) and they do Science: Biology, Chemistry and Physics. And they each do two creative subjects: they can choose from Music, Technology and Drama. But there's more.

'The school's got lots of extra-curricular things too – especially clubs,' says Nadia. 'If we want to, we can do all kinds of different activities. For example, there's a horse-riding club and a gymnastics club. Lots of the clubs meet at lunchtime, but some of them are after-school clubs.'

Caroline says, 'We can choose from lots of things. There's a theatre group, and a school orchestra. I'm in the orchestra – I play the trombone.'

'My favourite club is the pottery club,' says Sarah. 'I love doing artistic things. But I'm in the sailing club, too. The boys from the boys' school come to this club too. We learn about sailing during the week, and then some weekends we sail on a lake near here.'

Teachers organise some of the clubs at the school. Some clubs get help from parents of children at the school. All of them are free.

'I think the clubs are a really good idea,' says Nadia. 'We have a lot of fun and we learn different things.'

Sarah agrees. 'We can develop our own interests and hobbies in the clubs. I hope that we can start a photography club soon!'

10 Write

a Imagine that Lisa is your new e-pal and this is her first message to you. Read her message. What are her hobbies and interests?

from: lisa.franklin@kidsbox.co.uk

subject: Hello!

Hi!

I'm Lisa Franklin. I'm British and I live in Southampton. I'm 15.

I love sports. My favourite hobby is painting. I also like taking photographs (I'm in a photography club at school) and I enjoy riding my bike. I love watching sport on TV, especially tennis! I really like Rafael Nadal.

My best friend is Sonia. We listen to music a lot, and we often go to the cinema together too. Her favourite actor is Ben Stiller. I think he's very funny, but my favourite actor is Johnny Depp.

Write soon!

Lisa

c ► CD1 T11 Read the text again and listen. Write *T* (true) or *F* (false).

1 Sarah, Caroline and Nadia are all 14 years old.
2 They don't study languages.
3 All the clubs meet after school.
4 Caroline plays the trombone in the school orchestra.
5 Sarah is in a sailing club.
6 The girls' parents organise all the school clubs.
7 Their parents have to pay for the girls to be in a club.
8 There is a photography club at the school.

d Is this school similar to yours, or very different? Discuss this question with a partner or in small groups.

b Write an email in reply to Lisa. Include this information:

● your name, nationality and age
● where you live
● your hobbies and interests
● some information about your friend(s).

11 Speak

a Work with a partner. Think of five questions that you would like to ask Sarah from Park School.

b Work with your partner: one of you is the interviewer, the other one is Sarah. Ask and answer your questions.

For your portfolio

Helping other people

* Present continuous for activities happening now
* Present simple vs. present continuous
* Vocabulary: housework

1 Read and listen

a Give any examples you can of people who do 'volunteer work' (work you do without being paid).

b Look at the photos. How old do you think Mike is? Where is he and what is he doing? Read the text quickly and check your ideas.

c ▶ CD1 T12 Read the text again and listen. Mark the statements T (true) or F (false).

1 Mike usually lives in England. ☐
2 Mike is training to become a doctor. ☐
3 Mike is unhappy because he doesn't get any money. ☐
4 Mike is living in a house with five other people. ☐
5 Mike wants to go home when he finishes his work. ☐

d Answer the questions.

1 Why does Mike like what he is doing?
2 Say three places in the world where you would like to work as a volunteer.
3 Give an example of: a) volunteer work you would like to do; b) volunteer work you would not like to do.

Helping at a hospital

Every year many young people in Britain finish school and then take a year off before they start work or go to university. Some of them go to other countries and work as volunteers. Volunteers give their time to help people – for example, they work in schools or hospitals, or they help with conservation.

Mike Coleman is 19 and lives in Canterbury in England. He wants to become a teacher, but now he's living in Namibia. He's working in a hospital near Katima Mulilo. He says, 'I'm working with the doctors and nurses here to help sick people. I'm not a doctor but I can do a lot of things to help – for example, I help to carry people who can't walk. Sometimes I go to villages in the mobile hospital, too. There aren't many doctors here so they need help from people like me. I don't get any money – but that's OK, I'm not here for the money.

I'm staying here for two months and I'm living in a small house with five other volunteers. The work is hard and the days are long but I'm enjoying my life here. I'm learning a lot about life in southern Africa – and about myself! When I finish the two months' work, I want to travel in and around Namibia for three weeks – for example, I want to see the animals in the Okavango Delta in Botswana.'

ANGOLA   ZAMBIA
Katima Mulilo ☐
NAMIBIA
● Windhoek   BOTSWANA
SOUTH AFRICA

2 Grammar

✴ Present continuous for activities happening now

RULE: We use the present .... to talk about things that are happening at or around the time of speaking.

We form the present continuous with the present tense of .... + verb + *ing*.

a Look at the examples. Then complete the rule and the table.

*He's **working** in a hospital near Katima Mulilo.*
*I'm **living** in a small house with five other volunteers.*
*I'm **learning** a lot about life in southern Africa.*

Positive	Negative	Questions	Short answers
I'm (am) working	I'm not working	.... I working?	Yes, I **am**. No, I'm **not**.
you/we/they're (...............) working	you/we/they **aren't** working	.... you/we/they working?	Yes, you/we/they .... No, you/we/they ....
he/she/it's (is) working	he/she/it .... working	.... he/she/it working?	Yes, he/she/it .... No, he/she/it ....

b Complete the sentences. Use the present continuous form of the verbs.

1   Sorry, Eddie isn't here. He *'s taking* (take) the dog for a walk.

2   Mike and Jane are in the living room. They .... (watch) a film on DVD.

3   Hannah! You .... (not listen) to me!

4   I can't talk now. I .... (do) my homework.

5   **A:** .... you .... (watch) this programme?   **B:** No, I'm not. Watch a different one if you want.

6   **A:** Maddy's upstairs in her room.   **B:** Oh? Really? .... she .... (have) a rest?

c Look at the pictures and complete the sentences with the present continuous. Use the phrases in the box.

> listen to music   win   ~~have a rest~~   not enjoy this programme   not do her homework   watch television

1   My grandfather
    is having a rest .

2   Look! Our dog Max
    .... !

3   My parents
    ....

4   I ....

5   It's a great game – and
    we .... !

6   Ellie ....

3 Pronunciation

▶ **CD1 T13 and T14**   Turn to page 110.

4 Grammar

✱ Present simple vs. present continuous

a Look at the examples. Then (circle) the correct words in the sentences.

Present Simple	Present Continuous
Mike **lives** in Canterbury, England.	At the moment, h**e's living** in a house in Namibia.
Many people **work** as volunteers.	Mike **is working** in a hospital at the moment.
It often **snows** here.	Look outside – it**'s snowing**!

1 We (always wear) / We're always wearing a uniform to school.

2 Paula wears / Paula's wearing black jeans today.

3 Come inside! It rains / It's raining.

4 It rains / It's raining a lot in February.

5 Dad cooks / Dad's cooking at the moment.

6 My mother cooks / My mother's cooking lunch every Sunday.

7 Steve's terrible! He never listens / He's never listening to the teacher!

LOOK!

These verbs are almost never used in the present continuous:

believe   know   understand   want   remember   need   mean   like   hate

I **know** the answer. (Not: I'm knowing).
My friend **likes** rap music. (Not: My friend is liking).

b We use different time expressions with the two tenses. Complete the lists with the time expressions in the box.

at the moment   usually   every weekend
this afternoon   never   right now   today
every evening   this week   twice a year

Present simple	Present continuous
every day	now
always	this morning
....	....
....	....
....	....
....	....
....	....

c Complete the sentences. Use the present simple or present continuous form of the verbs.

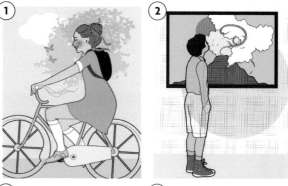

1 Sarah usually ___walks___ (walk) to school, but today she _____ (go) by bike.

2 We _____ (have) geography lessons twice a week. We _____ (learn) about volcanoes at the moment.

3 Julia _____ (surf) the net this afternoon. She _____ (want) to find some information for a project.

4 I _____ (know) his face, but I _____ (not remember) his name.

5 We _____ (not dance) tonight because we _____ (not like) the music.

6 What _____ this word _____ (mean)? I _____ (not understand) it.

5 Listen

a ▶ CD1 T15 Listen to a radio interview with Mike Coleman. What is he doing at the time of the interview? Choose the correct picture.

(1)

(2)

(3)

b ▶ CD1 T15 Listen again and write *T* (true) or *F* (false).

1 Mike has breakfast at about eight o'clock. ☐
2 Mike and his friends make breakfast, lunch and dinner. ☐
3 Mike uses a washing machine to do the washing. ☐
4 Mike sometimes cleans the floors and windows at the hospital. ☐
5 Mike is working with boring people. ☐

> **LOOK!**
> do the washing-up /
> wash up = wash dishes
> do the washing = wash clothes

6 Vocabulary

✱ Housework

▶ CD1 T16 Match the words with the pictures. Write 1–7 in the boxes. Then listen, check and repeat.

1 do the cooking
2 do the ironing
3 do the washing
4 do the shopping
5 do the washing-up / wash up
6 tidy up / tidy a room
7 clean the windows

Vocabulary bank Turn to page 112.

7 Speak

a Work in a group. Ask and answer questions about housework.

Do you help at home? Do you tidy your own room?
How often do you do the shopping / the washing-up ... ?
Which jobs do you like? Which do you hate?

b In your home, who usually does the housework? You, your brother or sister, your mother, your father? Compare with a partner.

My father usually does the cooking, but my mother always does the washing-up ...

Let's give him a hand

8 ▶ CD1 T17 Read and listen

a Look at the photostory. What do Jess, Joel and Pete do? Why do you think Debbie doesn't help? Read and listen to find the answers.

①

Jess: Hey, look at that guy.

Pete: Yeah. Let's give him a hand. Come on, Debbie.

Debbie: Not me. It's not my problem. Let *him* push his old car.

Joel: Well, I'm going to help him.

②

Pete: Come on! One, two, three – push!

Jess: Wow, it's heavy!

Joel: Yes, it is. It's moving, though!

③

Pete: We did it!

Joel: But he drove away! And he didn't even say 'Thank you'!

Pete: That's right. That's not very nice, is it?

④

Debbie: See? Told you! You're mad.

Jess: Why?

Debbie: Oh come on Jess! The man didn't even say 'Thank you'!

Jess: So what? We pushed the car to *help* him – not to hear him say 'Thank you'.

b Match the beginnings and endings to make a summary of the story.

1 A man	a want to help him.
2 Pete, Joel and Jess	b but he doesn't say 'Thank you'.
3 Debbie thinks	c needs help to start his car.
4 The car is heavy, but	d that 'Thank you' isn't important.
5 The man drives away	e they push it and it starts.
6 Jess thinks	f that it's the man's problem, not hers.

9 Everyday English

a Find expressions 1–6 in the photostory. Who says them?

1 It's not my problem.
2 Come on!
3 ..., though.
4 That's right.
5 See?
6 So what?

b Read the dialogue. Use the expressions in Exercise 9a to complete it.

Linda: What time does the film start? 8 o'clock?

Paul: ¹ *That's right* .

Linda: Well, we're late. ² _____, Paul! Let's go.

Paul: Late? No, we aren't late. Look at my watch. ³ _____? It's only six thirty.

Linda: Oh yes. OK, so we don't need to leave now. I don't want to be late, ⁴ _____ . Everyone says it's a really good film! And Ashton Kutcher's in it.

Paul: ⁵ _____? Ashton Kutcher isn't very good!

Linda: Not very good? You just don't understand acting. Well, ⁶ _____ – you don't have to come!

Discussion box

1 Debbie says the others are 'mad' because they helped the driver. What is your opinion?

2 In what situations do you find it easy or difficult to ask other people for help? Give your reasons.

3 When did you last help someone who had a problem? Say what happened.

10 Improvisation

Work with a partner. Take two minutes to prepare a short role play. Try to use some of the expressions from Exercise 9a. Do not write the text, just agree on your ideas for a short scene. Then act it out.

Roles: Debbie and the car driver

Situation: In the street – the next day

Basic idea: Debbie and the driver see each other in the street the next day.

Use one of these sentences to start the conversation:

Debbie: Excuse me, I think I know you. We pushed your car yesterday.

Man: Hi! Can I talk to you for a minute? I'd just like to say I'm sorry ...

11 Team Spirit ⊙ DVD Episode 1

a What's happening in the situation in the photo? What is the teacher going to say?

b Match the words with their definitions. Then watch Episode 1 and meet Jess, Pete, Debbie and Joel.

1 community service
2 badge
3 award
4 guest
5 bracelet
6 fashion designer

a a person who creates beautiful clothes

b a person who comes to a place because they are invited

c a piece of jewellery worn around the wrist or arm

d work that people do without payment to help other people

e a prize given to a person for doing something very well

f a small piece of metal or plastic that you can pin on your clothing

For your portfolio

12 Write

a Read Maggie's email to her friend about a family party. Answer the questions.

1 What is the event and when is it happening?

2 How many people are coming?

3 What is everybody doing to help?

b Imagine you are helping to prepare for one of these events:

- a family party
- a birthday celebration for one of your friends
- a goodbye party for your teacher

Write an email to a friend and tell him/her what is happening.

Hi Joanna,

How are things? Hope you're well.

This is going to be a quick message because I'm really busy. We're getting ready for my sister's 18th birthday. There's going to be a big party in the garden tonight – about 50 people are coming! So we're all here, cleaning and cooking and things. My mum's in the kitchen preparing food, and my dad's helping her. My sister Gill and my brother Alex are putting up a big tent and some lights in the garden, and some of my sister's friends are putting out the tables and chairs. My grandparents aren't helping – they're having a rest in their room. Well, sorry, I have to go – my mum's calling me. She needs some help!

Have a good weekend!

See you soon.

Maggie

---

13 Last but not least: more speaking

a ▶ CD1 T18 Read the phone call between Monique and her friend Tanya. Complete the dialogue using the verbs in the box in their correct form. Then listen and check.

study ~~speak~~ help do think tidy

Monique: Hi, Tanya. It's Monique _speaking_.

Tanya: Oh, hi, Monique. How are you?

Monique: Fine, thanks, and you?

Tanya: Yeah, I'm OK. A bit busy right now.

Monique: Busy? What are you [1] _____?

Tanya: Well, I'm [2] _____ my brother with his maths homework, but I'm also [3] _____ my room ...

Monique: What else?

Tanya: I'm [4] _____ about what I can get James for his birthday.

Monique: You know what, Tanya? Let's meet in Parker Square in half an hour and go to the shops together. We can look for a present for James there.

Tanya: Sorry, Monique, I can't.

Monique: No? What a pity! Why's that?

Tanya: I'm also [5] _____ for my English test too. It's tomorrow!

Monique: Oh no!

b Look at the dialogue with a partner. Think of some changes to make to the dialogue (names, for example), so that it becomes your dialogue. Act out the new dialogue in pairs. (Don't just read it out!)

Check your progress

1 Grammar

a Complete the sentences. Use the present simple form of the verbs.

1 You should read more, Jane. You __watch__ (watch) too much TV.
2 My uncle .... (live) in that house over there.
3 .... you .... (like) listening to CDs?
4 Alex and Sarah .... (play) computer games every weekend.
5 My father .... (not like) the same music as me.
6 Our teacher hardly ever .... (give) us a lot of homework.
7 A: .... your mother .... (work) on Saturdays?
   B: Yes, she ....
8 A: .... they .... (write) a lot of emails?
   B: No, they ....
9 I .... (not get up) early at the weekend.

`10`

b Complete the sentences. Use the present simple or present continuous form of the verbs.

1 Annie often __plays__ (play) football, but now she __'s playing__ (play) computer games.
2 My mum usually .... (work) in London, but this week she .... (work) in New York.
3 I .... (read) a magazine at the moment. It's strange, because I usually .... (not read) magazines.
4 We .... (not watch) television very often, but we .... (watch) an interesting programme at the moment.
5 A: .... your friends always .... (swim) in the sea?
   B: No, not always. They .... (swim) in the pool today.
6 A: Karen's not in her room. .... she .... (help) Dad in the kitchen?
   B: No, she .... (be) . She .... (have) a shower.

`11`

2 Vocabulary

a Put the letters in order to find nine more school subjects.

1 usMci   __Music__
2 marDa   ....
3 sthMa   ....
4 shinglE   ....
5 niecSec   ....
6 ortHiys   ....
7 rnecFh   ....
8 agGyehorp   ....
9 logonyeTch   ....
10 yesCmtrih   ....   `9`

b Write the words and phrases in the lists. Then add three more to each list.

doing the ironing   ~~listening to music~~
dancing   cleaning the windows
tidying up   playing the guitar

Hobbies and interests	Housework
listening to music	....
....	....
....	....
....	....
....	....
....	....

`11`

How did you do?

Check your score.

Total score	😊	😐	☹
`41`	Very good	OK	Not very good
Grammar	18 – 21	15 – 17	less than 15
Vocabulary	15 – 20	10 – 14	less than 10

Who's your hero?

* Past simple: *be* and regular verbs (positive and negative); *was born / were born*
* Vocabulary: multi-word verbs (1), memory words

1 Read and listen

a Look at the photos and the title. Why do you think this woman is a hero for some people? Read the text quickly and check your ideas.

Erin Brockovich

Erin Brockovich, an American woman, was born in Kansas. She studied at a business college for a year, then she moved to southern California and married a restaurant manager.

In 1990, when she was thirty years old, she was in a car accident. A law company helped her after the accident, and later she started to work for them.

Her job was to organise papers. One day Erin realised that there were lots of papers about some very sick people in a place called Hinkley. She started to look for more information about the town.

Erin worked very hard for five years. She visited lots of sick people in Hinkley and listened to their stories. All the people lived near a big Pacific Gas and Electric factory and she discovered that there was a chemical called chromium in the local water. It was from the factory and Erin believed that the people were sick because of the chromium in their drinking water. She planned to help them.

Erin and her boss started a law case against the Pacific Gas and Electric company. The company wasn't happy about this. They didn't agree that the people were ill because of the water – but in 1996 the judge ordered Pacific Gas and Electric to pay the people in Hinkley $500,000 each (there were 600 sick people, so that was $333 million in total).

In 2000, there was a film about Erin Brockovich. Julia Roberts played Erin and the film was very successful. Now Erin is famous – she has her own company and she gives talks all over the world.

b ▶ CD1 T19 Now read the text again and listen. Answer the questions.

1 What was Erin's job at the law company?
2 Why did Erin start to look for more information about Hinkley?
3 Where did the sick people in Hinkley live?
4 What was Erin's theory about why the people were sick?
5 How much money did Pacific Gas and Electric pay to people in Hinkley?
6 What does Erin Brockovich do now?

c Do you think the people in Hinkley were happy with the result of the law case?

Handwritten note: was = I

were = + I

2 Grammar

✳ Past simple: be

a Look at the text on page 26. Underline examples of the past simple of the verb *be*.

b Complete the table.

Handwritten: wasn't

Positive	Negative	Question	Short answer
I/he/she/it **was**	I/he/she/it **wasn't** (was not)	**was** I/he/she/it?	Yes, I/he/she/it **wasn't** No, I/he/she/it ___ (was **not**).
you/we/they **were**	you/we/they **weren't** (were not)	**were** you/we/they?	Yes, you/we/they **we are not** No, you/we/they ___ (were **not**).

c Complete the sentences with *was*, *wasn't*, *were* or *weren't*.

1 In 1990, Erin ___*was*___ in a car accident.

2 A lot of people in Hinkley __was__ sick.

3 The drinking water in Hinkley *Wasn't →* ~~_____~~ clean.

4 There __was__ chromium in the water.

5 The bosses at Pacific Gas and Electric __wasn't__ happy.

d Complete the questions with *Was* or *Were*.

1 ___*Was*___ Erin Brockovich British?

2 __Were (was)__ it her job to drive a car for the law company?

3 __Were__ there lots of papers about sick people in Hinkley?

4 __Were (was)__ the water in Hinkley clean?

5 __Was (ere)__ a lot of people in Hinkley sick?

6 __Were (was)__ the film *Erin Brockovich* successful?

e Work with a partner. Ask and answer the questions in Exercise 2d.

A: *Was Erin Brockovich British?*

B: *No, she wasn't. She was American.*

3 Pronunciation

▶ CD1 T20, T21 and T22   Turn to page 110.

4 Grammar

✳ was born / were born

Look at the example. Complete the sentences with your information.

Erin Brockovich was born in 1960. She was born in the USA.

1 I was born in __1998__ (year).

2 I was born in _____ (place).

5 Speak

a Ask other students.

When were you born?
Where were you born?

b Work with a partner. Ask and answer about family members. Complete the table for your partner's family.

A: *When was your sister born?*

B: *In 1998. Where were your parents born?*

A: *My mother was born in Rome and my father …*

Name	Year	Place
Grandfather		

6 ⬤ Grammar

✱ Past simple: regular verbs

a Look back at the text on page 26. Find the past simple form of these verbs.

study	_studied_
marry	....
help	....
start	....
realise	....
visit	....
live	....
believe	....
plan	....
order	....

b Look at the verbs in Exercise 6a. Complete the rule.

RULE: We use the past simple to talk about finished actions in the past.

With regular verbs, we usually add .... to the verb (*work – worked*, *start – started*).

If the verb ends in *e* (for example, *live*), we add ....

If a short verb ends in one vowel + consonant (for example, *plan*), we double the .... and add *ed*.

If the verb ends in consonant + *y* (for example, *study*), we change the *y* to .... and add ....

c Complete the sentences. Use the past simple form of the verbs.

1 Last night, I _studied_ (study) for today's test.
2 There was no food in the house, so we .... (order) a pizza.
3 I .... (want) to go to the cinema, and my friend Alex .... (agree) to come with me.
4 I .... (try) to phone my friend on Saturday, but no-one .... (answer).
5 Last year we .... (visit) my aunt and uncle in Australia.
6 My father .... (stop) watching TV and .... (help) me with my homework.

d Look at the example and complete the table.

*The company **didn't agree** that the people were ill because of the water.*

Positive	Negative
I/you/he/she/it/we/they want**ed**	I/you/he/she/it/we/they .... want

e Complete the sentences. Use the past simple form of the verbs in the box.

~~start~~   talk   tidy   stay   rain   study   not clean
~~not finish~~   not like   not watch   not play   not say

1 I _started_ a painting but I _didn't finish_ it.
2 They .... in an expensive hotel, but they .... the food.
3 It .... all day on Saturday, so we .... tennis.
4 Helena .... TV last night. She .... for her test.
5 I .... my room, but I .... the windows.
6 He .... for a long time, but he .... anything interesting!

7 Listen

a Pete made a poster about his hero for a class presentation. Look at the poster and the sentences. How many of the sentences can you complete?

b ▶ CD1 T23 Listen to Pete's presentation. Find information to complete the other sentences in the poster.

c Why is Dorothy Stang Pete's hero?

8 Vocabulary

✷ Multi-word verbs (1)

a Look at the examples from the listening.

*Can you **come up** here please?*
*A lot of people wanted to **cut down** the trees.*

Think of other verbs you know that end with *up* or *down*.

b ▶ CD1 T24 Match the sentences with the pictures. Then listen, check and repeat.

1 Climb up!
2 Pick it up, please!
3 Put them on!
4 Get in!
5 Take it off!
6 Come down!
7 Get out!
8 Put it down!

c Look at the verbs in Exercise 8b. Match them with their opposites.

climb up – come down

d Work with a partner. Think of different situations where you can use the verbs in Exercise 8b.

Vocabulary bank Turn to page 113.

MY HERO –
DOROTHY
STANG

born: 1931 in USA

decided to change her life

moved to Brazil

wanted to protect the trees in the rainforest

died in 2005

Anapú

PARÁ

BRAZIL

Brasília ●

1 Dorothy Stang was born in _____ , in Dayton, Ohio, USA.
2 She moved to Brazil in _____ .
3 Pará is in the _____ of Brazil.
4 She was *Woman of the Year* in Pará in _____ .
5 She died on the _____ of _____ , 2005.
6 The men who killed her are in _____ now.

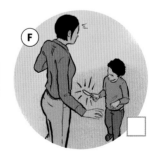

9 Read and listen

a Look at the photos. Do you know where these things are?

b ▶ CD1 T25 Read the text quickly and listen. Check your ideas.

REMEMBERING HEROES

Countries, cities and people all have their own heroes. There are different kinds of heroes: politicians, soldiers, film stars, sport stars and musicians. And there are many different ways of remembering them, too. Here are some of the things that we do to make sure that we don't forget our heroes.

- Sometimes we build statues or sculptures of heroes, especially of politicians and soldiers, but sometimes of writers too. Many cities in South America have a statue of Simón Bolívar (he helped lead many South American countries to independence). And the famous Mount Rushmore in the USA remembers four US presidents of the past.

- We often remember soldiers and other people who died in war with a monument, like the Monument to the People's heroes in Beijing, China, or a memorial, like the Eternal Flame at the Tomb of the Unknown Soldier in Paris.

- Some countries have a special remembrance day, like the one every January in the USA for Dr Martin Luther King, the human rights leader.

- When Lady Diana Spencer died in 1997, in Paris, many people left flowers and messages near the place where the car accident happened. Now there is a Diana, Princess of Wales Memorial Fountain in Hyde Park in London.

- Sometimes places are named after famous people: for example, Liverpool, in England and Rio de Janeiro, in Brazil both have airports named after local musicians, John Lennon and Tom Jobim.

- In Hollywood, The Walk of Fame has the names of film, TV and music celebrities in stars on the pavement. Very famous celebrities have their handprints, footprints and autographs in concrete at Hollywood's Grauman's Chinese Theatre.

Different countries and people remember their heroes in different ways, including many ways that are not mentioned here. Perhaps in your country there are some different ways – what are they?

c Read the text again and:

1 give four examples of different kinds of 'heroes'.

2 give an example of a statue to remember a hero.

3 say when *Martin Luther King Day* is.

4 give two examples of places named after famous people.

5 say what the *Walk of Fame* is.

d Work in pairs or groups. Answer the questions.

1 Which of the people in the text did you already know about?

2 What other ways can you think of to remember heroes?

3 How are heroes remembered in your country?

10 Vocabulary

✱ Memory words

Use a word from the box to complete each sentence.

> forget   unforgettable   ~~memories~~   memory
> remember   memorial   forgetful

1 I have lots of great *memories* of our holiday last year.

2 It was a fantastic day – I'll always ＿＿＿＿ it.

3 My brother has an amazing ＿＿＿＿ for names and faces.

4 When you finish using the computer, don't ＿＿＿＿ to switch it off.

5 There's a new statue in our town – it's a ＿＿＿＿ to a famous writer from our country.

6 My friend Allie didn't remember my birthday, or his sister's birthday! He's so ＿＿＿＿ .

7 We went to Paris last weekend. We had a great time – it was an ＿＿＿＿ holiday.

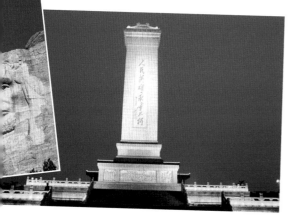

11 Write

a Read the text that Dave wrote about his hero. Match the questions with the paragraphs. Write numbers 1–3 in the boxes.

a What did this person do? ☐

b Why is this person a hero for you? ☐

c Who is your hero? ☐

1 My hero is Helen Thayer. She was the first woman to walk to the magnetic North Pole alone.

2 Helen Thayer was born in New Zealand and she lived there when she was a girl. Later, she lived in Guatemala for four years and then in the United States. When she was fifty, she had a dream. She wanted to walk to the North Pole alone, and she decided to do it. On her journey, Helen didn't have any help. She was completely alone except for her dog, Charlie, a Canadian husky. The journey was very difficult. She walked 345 miles in temperatures of −50 °C! Once, seven polar bears attacked Helen and Charlie. Charlie saved Helen's life.

3 Helen Thayer is my hero because she had a dream and she was determined to make it come true. She was always positive, even in very dangerous and difficult situations.

b Think of someone you think is a hero. Write three paragraphs about your hero. Use Dave's example to help you.

12 Speak

Make a poster about your hero. Then give a presentation to the class.

For your portfolio

4 Making friends

* Past simple (regular and irregular verbs; questions and short answers)
* Vocabulary: past time expressions, sports

1 Read and listen

a How many sports do you know in English? What is your favourite sport?

b Read about two sportsmen at a World Championship in 1971. What nationalities were the two men? What was their sport?

c ▶ CD1 T26 Now read the text again and listen. Put the pictures in the correct order. Write numbers 1–5 in the boxes.

The ping pong friendship that changed the world

Many years ago In 1971, the US table tennis team was at the World Championship in Japan. The team from the People's Republic of China was also there. This championship took place during the days of the Cold War and so the American and the Chinese players didn't even talk to each other.

Glen Cowan, from the US team, didn't like the situation. One day, he saw a Chinese player and invited him to play. They played together for 15 minutes, and Cowan missed the US bus back to the hotel.

Then, something surprising happened. One of the Chinese players waved to Cowan from the Chinese bus. He thought for a moment – and then he got on the bus. But the Chinese players didn't talk to him. Suddenly Zhuang Zedong, three times world champion, came up to Cowan. 'What are you doing?' said the other Chinese players. 'Don't talk to him! Don't make trouble!' Zedong gave Cowan a silk scarf. 'I give you this to show the friendship of the Chinese people to the American people,' he said through a translator. Cowan wanted to give something back, but he didn't have anything with him.

Then the bus arrived at the hotel. There were lots of reporters – it was big news to see an American and a Chinese player together.

Later, Cowan bought a T-shirt with a peace flag on it, and he gave it to Zedong. The two men became friends.

In the same year, the US team got an invitation to visit China, and in February 1972, US President Richard Nixon went to China on a historic visit. Many people say that the two men and their friendship made a better relationship between their countries possible.

d Answer the questions.

1 Why didn't the American and Chinese players talk to each other?

2 Why did Cowan get on the Chinese team bus?

3 Why didn't Cowan give Zedong a present immediately?

4 Why were there reporters at the hotel when the bus arrived?

e Do you think that Zedong and Cowan stayed friends for a long time? Why/why not?

2 Grammar

✱ Past simple: regular and irregular verbs

a Look at the examples from the text on page 32. How are the verbs in 1 different from the verbs in 2?

1 *They **played** for fifteen minutes.*
*He **wanted** to give something back*
*The bus **arrived** at the hotel.*

2 *He **got on** the Chinese bus.*
*Zedong **gave** him a scarf.*
*The US president **went** to China.*

b Put the verbs from the box in the past simple and write them in the lists. Use the text on page 32 to help you.

change	see	call	play	miss
think	get	come	give	want
arrive	buy	become	make	

Regular verbs	Irregular verbs
changed	*saw*

c Complete the summary. Use the past simple form of the verbs.

There [1] _was_ (be) a table tennis championship in Japan in 1971. An American and a Chinese player [2] _____ (play) together for fifteen minutes. The American [3] _____ (miss) his bus, but the Chinese player [4] _____ (invite) him onto his bus.

The Chinese player [5] _____ (give) the American a present. The American [6] _____ (be) happy, and he [7] _____ (want) to give a present back. He [8] _____ (buy) a T-shirt for the Chinese player. They [9] _____ (become) friends.

In the same year, the American President [10] _____ (go) to China for a historic visit.

✱ Past simple: questions

d Look at the examples and complete the table.

*Did the Chinese players **talk** to Cowan? No, they **didn't**.*
*Did Cowan and Zedong **become** friends? Yes, they **did**.*

Question	Short answer
_____ I/you/he/she/it/we/they go?	Yes, I/you/he/she/it/we/they _____ .
	No, I/you/he/she/it/we/they _____ (**did not**).

e Put the words in the correct order to make questions.

1 you / go out / last night / did ?

_____

2 music / you / on Sunday / did / listen to ?

_____

3 eggs / you / for breakfast / this morning / eat / did ?

_____

4 you / watch / last night / did / TV ?

_____

5 on holiday / you / last year / did / go ?

_____

3 Speak

Work with a partner. Ask and answer the questions from Exercise 2e.

A: *Did you go out last night?*

B: *No, I didn't. I stayed at home and watched TV.*

4 Vocabulary

★ Past time expressions

a When we talk about the past, we can use time expressions like these. Add another example to each list.

> yesterday, yesterday morning, yesterday _____
>
> last night, last week, last April, last _____
>
> an hour ago, four days ago, _____ ago

b Complete the sentences with your own information.

1 Four hours ago, I was _____
_____ .

2 Last night, I went to bed at
_____ .

3 Yesterday evening, I _____
_____ .

4 Last Saturday, I _____
_____ .

5 Eight years ago, I was _____
_____ .

6 My last holiday was _____
_____ .

c Complete the sentences. Use a time expression with *ago*.

1 David is fifteen now. He started school when he was five.
David started school
ten years ago .

2 I met your cousin last Saturday. It's Wednesday today.
I met your cousin _____ .

3 It's 10.30 now. My English class began at 9.30.
My English class began
_____ .

4 The school holidays started at the end of June. It's the end of August now.
The school holidays started
_____ .

5 Speak

Work in small groups. Ask and answer the questions. Use *ago* in your answers.

When / start school?   When / begin learning English?

When / arrive at school this morning?

When / first meet your best friend?

A: *When did you start school?*   B: *Nine years ago.*

6 Vocabulary

★ Sports

a ▶ CD1 T27 Write the words under the pictures. Then listen, check and repeat.

> ~~cycling~~ basketball ice hockey skateboarding
> snowboarding surfing swimming volleyball skiing

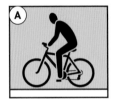
cycling

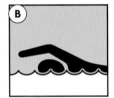
_____

_____

_____

_____

_____

_____

_____

_____

b Work with a partner or in a group. Answer the questions about the sports in Exercise 6a.

Which sports ...

1 are team sports?

2 use equipment with wheels?

3 are water sports?

4 are in the Winter Olympics?

5 are popular in your country?

6 do you do?

7 do you like watching?

Vocabulary bank Turn to page 113.

7 Pronunciation

▶ CD1 T28 Turn to page 110.

8 Listen

 Nick    Dan    Mr Stern    Mr Winter

a Look at the pictures of four people in a TV programme. Read their names.

b Look at the pictures from the story.

 A

 B

 C

 D

 E — Stern? No way!

 F

 G — 1

 H

1 What do you think the relationship is between the four people?

2 **CD1 T29** Put the pictures in order to tell a story. Then listen and check your ideas.

c Work with a partner. Re-tell the story. Use the pictures to help you.

9 Listen: a song

a Read the words of the song. Put the phrases in the box into the correct spaces.

> a little smarter than I am
> I've got them too
> from your nice warm bed
> We stick together

b **CD1 T30** Listen and check.

You've got a friend in me
Randy Newman

You've got a friend in me, you've got a friend in me.

When the road looks rough ahead

And you're miles and miles [1] _____

You just remember what your old pal said, boy,

You've got a friend in me.

Yeah, you've got a friend in me.

You've got a friend in me, you've got a friend in me.

If you've got troubles, [2] _____ .

There isn't anything I wouldn't do for you.

[3] _____ and we can see it through, 'cos

You've got a friend in me, yeah, you've got a friend in me.

Some other folks might be [4] _____ .

Bigger and stronger too, baby.

But none of them will ever love you the way I do.

It's me and you, boy.

And as the years go by, our friendship will never die.

You're gonna see, it's our destiny.

You've got a friend in me, you've got a friend in me,

Yeah, you've got a friend in me.

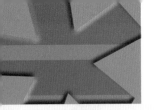

Not a nice thing to say

10 ► CD1 T31 **Read and listen**

a Look at the photostory. Who is unhappy? Who is he unhappy with? Read and listen to find the answers.

1

Joel: What have we got this afternoon?

Debbie: It's the cookery lesson. We're making cakes.

Pete: What about making cakes for the party on Saturday?

Jess: Nice one. Sounds good to me.

2

Debbie: But don't let Pete make any cakes!

Pete: Why not?

Debbie: Don't you remember? That time at your place when you made pizza for us? It was horrible!

Pete: It wasn't that bad! And you ate it, I remember!

3

Joel: *Not* a very nice thing to say, Debbie.

Debbie: Oh, Joel. I was only joking. Can't we make jokes about friends?

Jess: Yes, Debbie. But on the other hand, real friends try not to hurt each other.

Debbie: OK. I'm sorry I hurt you, Pete. I didn't mean to.

Pete: Never mind. Let's forget about it. OK guys – see you all tomorrow.

Debbie: Oh dear – he isn't very happy, is he?

Jess: No, I don't think so. And to be honest, I'm not surprised.

4

b Complete the sentences with the names: *Debbie, Pete, Jess,* or *Joel.*

1 __Pete__ suggests making cakes for the party.

2 _____ says Pete made an awful pizza one time.

3 _____ gets a bit angry.

4 _____ tells Debbie that she wasn't very friendly.

5 _____ says it's OK to make jokes about friends.

6 _____ says real friends don't hurt each other.

7 _____ says sorry to Pete.

8 _____ thinks it's natural that Pete isn't happy.

11 Everyday English

a Find expressions 1–6 in the photostory. Who says them?

1. What about … ?
2. on the other hand, …
3. I didn't mean to.
4. Never mind.
5. I don't think so.
6. to be honest, …

b Read the dialogues. Use the expressions in Exercise 11a to complete them.

1. A: Is Hannah German?
   B: ¹ *I don't think so* . I think she's from Austria.

2. A: ² .... going for a walk?
   B: Well, I'm a bit tired, so ³ .... , I don't want to go out.

3. A: Mrs Jones gave us a lot of homework, didn't she?
   B: Yes, a lot! But ⁴ .... , it's the weekend, so we've got 3 days to do it.

4. A: I'm sorry I broke your camera.
   ⁵ ....
   B: ⁶ .... It was an old camera anyway.

Discussion box

1. Pete is hurt when Debbie makes a joke about his cooking. How would you react in the same situation?

2. Debbie was 'only joking'. Discuss possible reasons why she was joking.

   A: *Maybe Debbie likes Pete, and that's why she made the joke.*

   B: *I'm not sure. I think she said it because …*

12 Improvisation

Work with a partner. Take two minutes to prepare a short role play. Try to use some of the expressions from Exercise 11a. Do not write the text, just agree on your ideas for a short scene. Then act it out.

Roles: Debbie and her mum

Situation: At home – later the same day

Basic idea: Debbie and her mum talk about Pete.

Use one of these sentences to start the conversation:

Debbie: Can I ask you something, Mum?

Mum: You don't look very happy today, Debbie. Is something wrong?

13 Team Spirit ⊙ DVD Episode 2

a Who are the people in the photo? How does each of them feel, and why, do you think?

b Jess, Debbie, Joel and Pete have agreed to meet. Suddenly Pete says he can't come. He doesn't give a reason. Work with a partner and write a story (of not more than 80 words) to explain why they wanted to meet and what happened.

c Read out your stories. Then watch Episode 2 and find out what happened.

For your portfolio

14 Write

Do one of these activities.

a Imagine you are Dan in the story on page 35. Write a diary entry for Dan about what happened.

Or

b Read Alison's email to her friend, Julia. Answer the questions.

1 Where did Alison go at the weekend?
2 What did she do there?
3 What does she ask Julia to send her?

Now write a similar email to a friend. Tell him/her about a weekend or day you enjoyed. Use Alison's email to help you.

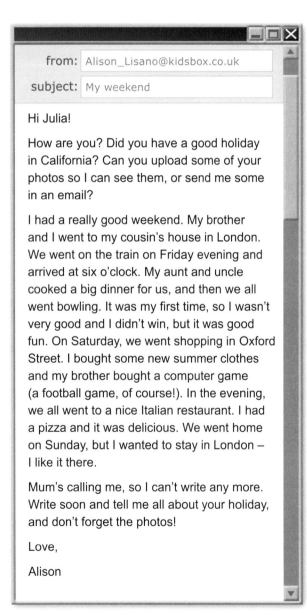

from: Alison_Lisano@kidsbox.co.uk

subject: My weekend

Hi Julia!

How are you? Did you have a good holiday in California? Can you upload some of your photos so I can see them, or send me some in an email?

I had a really good weekend. My brother and I went to my cousin's house in London. We went on the train on Friday evening and arrived at six o'clock. My aunt and uncle cooked a big dinner for us, and then we all went bowling. It was my first time, so I wasn't very good and I didn't win, but it was good fun. On Saturday, we went shopping in Oxford Street. I bought some new summer clothes and my brother bought a computer game (a football game, of course!). In the evening, we all went to a nice Italian restaurant. I had a pizza and it was delicious. We went home on Sunday, but I wanted to stay in London – I like it there.

Mum's calling me, so I can't write any more. Write soon and tell me all about your holiday, and don't forget the photos!

Love,

Alison

15 Last but not least: more speaking

✱ Alibi – a game

a Two students (A and B) invent a story about what they did last Saturday from 4–7 pm. The other students cannot hear what they are saying.

b All the other students are detectives. They ask A questions (B can't listen) and take notes. When A doesn't know an answer, he/she has to invent one.

c Now the class asks B questions about what they did and tries to find 'mistakes' in the alibi.

Class: *Where were you at 6 pm?*

B: *We were at a football match.*

Class: *Who was with you?*

B: *My friend, Nick.*

Class: *Who played?*

B: *Manchester United and Chelsea.*

Class: *Mistake! [A] said Manchester United and Real Madrid. What happened … ?*

Check your progress

1 Grammar

a Complete the dialogue with the past simple form of *be*.

A: You [1] _weren't_ at school yesterday afternoon. Where [2] _____ you?

B: I [3] _____ at home. There [4] _____ a football match on television.

A: [5] _____ it a good match?

B: No, it [6] _____ ! All the players [7] _____ awful! `6`

b Complete the sentences. Use the past simple form of the verbs.

1 In 1950, there _were_ (be) 199,854 people at the World Cup Final between Brazil and Uruguay in Rio de Janeiro. They _____ (see) a great match – but Brazil _____ (not win).

2 The Swedish athlete Oskar Gomar Swann _____ (become) famous when he _____ (win) a silver medal in shooting at the Olympic Games in Antwerp in 1920. He _____ (be) 72 years old.

3 At the 1984 Olympic Games in Los Angeles, Carl Lewis _____ (win) four gold medals.

4 In the first round of the long jump, Lewis _____ (jump) 8.54 metres. After that, he _____ (stop). 'Nobody can beat me,' he _____ (say).

5 I _____ (go) to the cinema last night, but I _____ (not enjoy) the film very much.

6 A: What _____ James _____ (say) to you yesterday?

   B: He _____ (not say) anything!

7 A: _____ you _____ (see) Alice last night?

   B: No, I _____ (not see) Alice, but I _____ (see) Jenny.

8 A: Where_____ you _____ (go) last summer?

   B: We _____ (go) to New York. But we _____ (not go) up the Empire State Building. `19`

2 Vocabulary

a Complete the sentences with the words in the box.

> up   down   out   on   off

1 Let's go _out_ tonight. I don't want to stay at home.

2 Leo, look at all your books on the floor! Pick them _____ , please.

3 This bag is very heavy. I'm going to put it _____ for a minute.

4 It's cold today. You should put _____ a warm coat.

5 It's hot in here. I'm going to take my jumper _____ . `4`

b Fill in the puzzle with names of sports. What is the mystery word?

	1	s	n	o	w	b	o	a	r	d	i	n	g
2												
			3									
4											
			p								
5										
6										
7										

1 You do this on a board in snow.
2 You need six players, a ball and a net to play this game.
3 You need a bike for this sport.
4 You do this in a pool.
5 You do this in the mountains in winter.
6 Ice _____ is a winter team game.
7 You go to the sea with a board for this sport. `6`

How did you do?

Check your score.

Total score	🙂	😐	🙁
`35`	Very good	OK	Not very good
Grammar	19 – 25	16 – 18	less than 16
Vocabulary	8 – 10	6 – 9	less than 6

5 Successful people

* *have to / don't have to*
* Vocabulary: jobs, work and money

1 Read and listen

a Look at the photos. Match the people with the jobs. Write 1–4 in the boxes.

| 1 sports person | 2 actor | 3 business person | 4 TV show host |

What does 'success' mean?

All the people on this page are 'successful' in some way. They're very different people and they do different things – but what they have in common is 'success'.

But if we say, 'This person is successful', what do we really mean? Do we mean that the person is rich? Do we mean that she or he is famous and everybody recognises them in the street? Or do they have to be very, very good at the things that they do for us to say that they are 'successful'?

Some people say that 'success' is none of these things – it's just being happy, and it doesn't matter if you are rich or famous or not. After all, there are lots of 'successful' people who aren't very happy, and lots of happy people who aren't 'successful'.

What do you think?

Oprah Winfrey

People (even politicians) listen to her

Jeff Bezos

Wealthy creator of amazon.com

Johnny Depp

A famous face in many films

Ana Ivanovic

Number 1 women's tennis player in 2008

e ▶ CD1 T32 Listen to six teenagers talking about success. Which things in Exercise 1d does each one talk about?

Speaker 1 ....

Speaker 2 ....

Speaker 3 ....

Speaker 4 ....

Speaker 5 ....

Speaker 6 ....

b In what ways are the people above different? In what ways are they similar?

c Read the text quickly. Find three things that can mean 'success'.

d What do you think success means? Tick (✓) the things that you think are necessary for someone to be 'successful'. Then compare your ideas with a partner.

a	being famous	☐	e being intelligent	☐
b	being happy	☐	f doing what you want to do	☐
c	having lots of money	☐	g being good at what you do	☐
d	being respected	☐	h enjoying your life	☐

f Think of someone you know who is successful but not famous. In what ways is this person successful? Discuss your ideas with a partner.

2 Grammar

★ *have to / don't have to*

a Look at the examples from the reading and listening texts. Complete the rule and the table.

*You **have to** be good at what you do.* *You **don't have to** be famous to be successful.*
*You **don't have to** be intelligent.* *You **have to** enjoy your work.*

Positive	Negative	Question	Short answer
I/you/we/they **have to** go	I/you/we/they _____ **(do not) have to** go	_____ I/you/we/they **have to** go?	Yes, I/you/we/they _____ . No, I/you/we/they _____ **(do not)**.
he/she/it _____ go	he/she/it _____ **(does not) have to** go	_____ he/she/it **have to** go?	Yes, he/she/it _____ . No, he/she/it _____ **(does not)**.

RULE:

We use _____ to say 'This is necessary'.

We use _____ to say 'This isn't necessary'.

b Complete the sentences. Use *have/has to* or *don't/doesn't have to*.

1 If you want to work in the USA, you ___*have to*___ speak good English.

2 My sister has got a young baby, so she often _____ get up during the night.

3 My friend gets good test results, but he _____ work very hard. In fact, he never studies before a test.

4 Tomorrow is Sunday, so I _____ go to school. Great!

5 At our school, we _____ wear a uniform. It's dark blue with a white shirt.

6 At my cousins' school they _____ wear a uniform. They can wear what they want.

3 Pronunciation

 Turn to page 110.

4 Speak

a Write ✓ for the things you have to do at home. Write ✗ for the things you don't have to do.

A get up at the same time on Saturday as on weekdays

B do homework

C do housework

D do the cooking

E help in the garden

F look after (pets/brothers and sisters)

b Work with a partner. Ask and answer questions about the activities in Exercise 4a.

A: *At the weekend, do you have to get up at the same time as on weekdays?*

B: *No, I don't – but I can't stay in bed all day! What about you?*

A: *I can get up later, but I have to help in the garden on Sundays.*

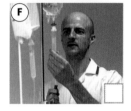

A *8*

5 Vocabulary

✱ Jobs

a ▶ CD1 T34 Match the names of the jobs with the pictures. Write 1–12 in the boxes. Then listen, check and repeat.

> 1 engineer 2 shop assistant 3 nurse
> 4 vet 5 doctor 6 flight attendant
> 7 lawyer 8 ~~pilot~~ 9 dentist
> 10 firefighter 11 teacher 12 architect

b Write the names of three more jobs you are interested in. Use a dictionary or ask your teacher.

1 ....

2 ....

3 ....

LOOK!

When we talk about jobs in English, we often use *a/an* before the job:
*My mother's **a nurse**.*
*I want to be **an engineer** when I leave school.*

c ▶ CD1 T35 Listen to four teenagers. Which job does each one want to do in the future? Fill in the spaces with four of the jobs in the box.

> pilot singer doctor
> teacher tennis player ~~vet~~
> computer programmer flight attendant

1 Luke: ....

2 Rose: ....

3 Sam: ....

4 Judith: ....

Vocabulary bank Turn to page 114.

6 Speak

a ▶ CD1 T36 Read the dialogue between two students. Fill in the spaces with the phrases from the box. Then listen and check your answers.

> speak English be a pilot not sure
> get good school results leave school
> I'd like Maths and Physics have to do

Jenny: What do you want to be when you ¹............. ?

Mark: I want to ²............. .

Jenny: Really? What do you ³............. for that?

Mark: You have to ⁴............. and you have to be good at ⁵............. . And you have to ⁶............. really well. What about you? What do you want to do?

Jenny: I'm ⁷............. , but I think ⁸............. to be a vet.

b Work with a partner. Continue the dialogue between Jenny and Mark. Use the phrases in the box. Then practise the whole dialogue.

> like animals study for five years
> get good results be good at Biology

c Work with a different partner. Find out about what he/she wants to be. Use the dialogue between Jenny and Mark to help you.

Read

a Look at the photos.

1 Do you know who the person is?

2 What is the sport?

3 Why do you think the text has the title *Following a dream*?

Read the text quickly and check your ideas.

b Read the text again. Answer the questions.

1 When did Hamilton's dream to be a Formula 1 driver begin?

2 What did he do when he was eight?

3 What did he tell Ron Dennis when he was ten?

4 Why did Ron Dennis phone Hamilton?

5 How old was Hamilton when he joined McLaren's programme?

6 What happened when Hamilton started driving in Formula 1 races?

c What do you know about Lewis Hamilton since 2008? Tell the class.

d Work in groups. Make a list of three people who became famous when they were young. Make notes about each of them. Then tell the others in the class about them and why you chose them.

FOLLOWING A DREAM

Lewis Hamilton's parents came to Britain from the island of Grenada in the 1950s. Lewis was born in 1985, and his parents named him after the American athlete Carl Lewis. Did they know that sporting fame was waiting for their son, too?

When Lewis was six, his father gave him a radio-controlled car and he began to win competitions, even against adults. From this very young age, Lewis' dream was to become a Formula 1 driver so his father bought him a go-kart and he started go-kart racing in 1993 when he was only eight years old. He won a couple of races, and he knew that he had to win more.

One day, when he was 10 years old, Lewis met a man called Ron Dennis. Dennis was the boss of the McLaren Formula 1 team. Lewis asked Dennis for his autograph, saying, 'My name's Lewis Hamilton and one day I want to drive your cars.' Ron Dennis wrote in his autograph book, 'Phone me nine years from now, we'll sort something out.' In fact, when Hamilton won his first go-kart championship a few years later, Ron Dennis phoned him, and in 1999 Hamilton joined McLaren's 'Young Drivers' programme. He was the youngest person ever to do this.

In 2001, world Formula 1 champion Michael Schumacher raced against Hamilton in a go-kart race and said, 'He's a quality driver, very strong and only 16. If he keeps this up, I'm sure he will reach F1.'

Schumacher was right. Lewis Hamilton started as a driver in F1 races in 2007. In his first six races, he came third, second, second, second, second and first. Then he came first again in his next race. He finished the season in second place, behind Kimi Räikkönen. Then in 2008, at the age of 23, Hamilton became the youngest world champion in F1 history when he finished one point ahead of Felipe Massa.

Lewis Hamilton had a dream, and he followed it and found what he wanted. And that's success!

UNIT 5   43

Culture in mind

8 Read and listen

a Match the words in the box with the photos and captions. Write 1–5 in the boxes.

> 1 washing cars   2 delivering newspapers   3 babysitting   4 dog-walking   5 helping elderly people

b ▶ CD1 T37   What do the five things have in common? Read the text quickly and check your ideas.

c Which job (or jobs) above involves:

1 water?
2 walking?
3 a bicycle?
4 carrying things?
5 going to another person's house?
6 animals?

d Put the five jobs in the text in order. 1 = the job you would like to do most, 5 = the job you would like to do least. Compare with a partner.

Teenagers: earning money

In many countries, you can only get a proper, full-time job if you are 16 or 18 years old. But there are things that teenagers in some places can do to earn some pocket money. Here are a few ideas.

Parents with a small child want to go out for the evening for dinner, or to the cinema, but they don't want to leave their child alone. So, they ask a teenager to stay in the house and look after him or her while they are out. And if the child's asleep, you can do your homework and not waste time!

Teenagers can deliver newspapers – usually you ride a bike around a neighbourhood and leave the newspaper at each house. Normally you have to have your own bike – and you have to get up early too, because people want their newspaper to read with their breakfast!

Some adults have a dog but they don't have time to take it for a walk. Dogs need a lot of exercise! So some teenagers work as dog-walkers. It's a good idea – you earn money and you're outside in the fresh air, getting some exercise too!

Lots of older people are happy for teenagers to help them carry their shopping or do small things in their home, like washing or ironing or keeping them company. You earn money, and people in the neighbourhood get your help.

They're all great ideas. Just choose one of them to earn some money. Then you can spend it or save it!

9 Vocabulary

✳ Work and money

a Complete each sentence with a word from the box.

> Saturday job earn full-time ~~part-time~~
> pocket money save spend waste

1 She only works two hours every morning – it's just a __part-time__ job.

2 When I've got some money, I always put it in the bank and _____ it.

3 I work every Saturday to _____ some money for myself.

4 I go to bed early on a Friday because I've got a _____ .

5 I like to _____ my money on clothes and CDs.

6 I don't work at all because my parents give me _____ every month.

7 That film is really awful – so don't _____ your money by going to see it!

8 My brother works 9–5, five days a week – it's a _____ job!

b What's the difference between:

1 a part-time job and a full-time job?

2 to earn money and to spend money?

3 to spend money and to save money?

4 to spend money and to waste money?

It's crazy for adults to drive to an expensive car wash when they can get a teenager to do the job for less money. Wash the car well and carefully and people will want you to do it again. Then you've got customers!

But don't forget it's important always to tell an adult where you're going. Be safe! Don't be stupid!

10 Speak

a Choose a job that you want to do when you leave school.

b List the good things about this job, and some 'not-so-good' things too, and think about why you want to have this job.

c Talk for about half a minute about the job.

11 Write

a Read the questions Hakan asked his uncle. Then read what he wrote about his uncle's job. Match the questions with the paragraphs. Write 1–3 in the boxes.

a What do you like and dislike about your job? ☐

b Why did you decide to be a dentist, and what did you have to do to get the job? ☐

c What do you have to do in your job? ☐

1 When he was young, my uncle Erol always wanted to be a policeman, but when he was 18, he decided to be a dentist because dentists earn more money. To be a dentist, he had to study hard for five years at university and take a lot of exams.

2 In his job, my uncle has to clean and fix people's teeth, and sometimes he has to pull them out! He doesn't have to get up very early but he has to work hard, usually from 10.00 in the morning to 7.30 in the evening from Monday to Saturday. It's a full-time job.

3 He likes his job because he never has to take his work home, and he meets lots of people. One thing he doesn't like is that he can't really talk to his patients because he is working inside their mouths!

b Ask a friend or family member about his/her job. Then write about it using the information you get. Use Hakan's questions and text to help you.

6 Eat for life

* Countable and uncountable nouns
* *a/an*, *some* and *any*, *much* and *many*
* Vocabulary: food and drink

1 Read and listen

a Think of things that can help people live a long time and compare with a partner. Then read the text quickly and check your ideas.

A long and healthy life

Everyone wants to be healthy and live a long time. But how can we do it? Some years ago, a 90-year-old American writer gave some advice for a long and healthy life:

* Believe in yourself.
* Keep your mind active.
* Be positive.
* Love people and enjoy helping others.

The women of Okinawa, in Japan, are another great example: they live a long time, they are very fit and they don't have many diseases or heart problems. Their secret? They do some exercise every day, they don't have much stress in their lives and, in general, they are positive and active.

But of course, diet is important, too. The Okinawa women eat tofu, fish, green vegetables, carrots, fruit, spices and sweet potatoes. They eat some meat, but they don't eat any fat from the meat. And they eat seaweed – this contains many different vitamins and minerals and is good for your heart.

The Mediterranean diet is very healthy, too. It consists of vegetables, tomatoes, lemons, fish, beans, garlic, cheese, yoghurt, rice and pasta. The fat in this diet is 'good fat': it comes from olive oil and from fish.

So, what do these two diets tell us?

* Don't eat any bad fats – like fats in sweets, fried food and meat.
* Eat healthy carbohydrates – vegetables, fruit, potatoes, rice.
* Don't use much oil in cooking. If you use oil, use a good one like olive oil. And avoid deep-fried food!
* If you're a little hungry, eat an apple or a carrot – not a packet of crisps!

Eat well, live an active and stress-free life – and you'll live a long time.

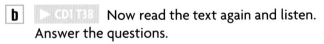

b ▶ CD1 T38 Now read the text again and listen. Answer the questions.

1 Does the American writer give advice for your mind or your body?
2 Why do the women in Okinawa live a long time?
3 Why is seaweed good for you?
4 Where does the fat come from in the Mediterranean diet?

c Do you know any people who are very old? Tell the class about them. Talk about their lifestyle and diet.

2 Vocabulary

✱ Food and drink

▶ CD1 T39 Write the words under the pictures. Then listen, check and repeat.

apples   carrots   eggs   meat   fruit
bread   ~~vegetables~~   tomatoes   orange juice
beans   onions   sugar   mineral water   rice

A   B   C   D   E   F   G

vegetables _____

H   I   J   K   L   M   N

_____

Vocabulary bank Turn to page 114.

3 Grammar

✱ Countable and uncountable nouns

a Read the rule. Then underline the countable nouns and (circle) the uncountable nouns in examples 1–4.

> **RULE:** In English, we can count some nouns: *one apple, two bananas, three carrots,* etc. We call these words *countable nouns.*
>
> There are some nouns we can't count, for example: *food* and *fruit.* These nouns have no plural. We call them *uncountable nouns.*

1   Eat an <u>apple</u> or a <u>carrot</u>.
2   They do some exercise every day.
3   Some years ago …
4   The Okinawa women eat fish and green vegetables.

b Complete the lists with words from Exercise 2.

Countable nouns	Uncountable nouns
vegetables	_fruit_

✱ *a/an* and *some*

c Look again at the examples in Exercise 3a. Complete the rule with *countable* or *uncountable*.

> **RULE:** We use *a/an* with singular _____ nouns. We use *some* with plural _____ nouns. We use *some* with _____ nouns.

d Complete the sentences with *a, an* or *some.*

1   I'd like __*some*__ sugar in my coffee.
2   I'm going to the shops. Mum needs _____ meat and _____ eggs.
3   This is _____ lovely apple!
4   _____ onion is _____ vegetable.
5   Have _____ fruit. There are _____ nice bananas in the kitchen.
6   She needs _____ bread, _____ cheese and _____ tomato to make a sandwich.
7   I'm a bit hungry – I think I'll eat _____ orange.

✱ *much* and *many*

e Look at the examples. Then complete the rule.

*Don't use **much** oil.*

*They don't have **many diseases** or **heart problems**.*

*How **many meals** do you have a day?*

*How **much water** do you drink?*

> **RULE:** We can use *much* and *many* in negative sentences and questions. We use *many* with plural _____ nouns. We use *much* with _____ nouns.

f (Circle) the correct words in questions 1–6. Then match the questions with the answers.

1   Is there (much) / *many* milk in the fridge?
2   How *much* / *many* potatoes do you want?
3   How *much* / *many* time have we got?
4   Are there *much* / *many* people in the café?
5   How *much* / *many* subjects do you study?
6   How *much* / *many* money have you got?

a   Yes, there are about 50.
b   €15.
c   No, there isn't.
d   Two, please.
e   Ten minutes.
f   Nine.

4 Speak

a Work with a partner. Discuss the quiz questions and choose the answers you think are correct.

b Ask your partner about the things in the quiz. For example:

Do you eat a lot of hamburgers?

How many hamburgers do you eat every month?

How often do you eat an apple?

1 How many calories are there in an average hamburger?

A 150   B 220   C 280

2 How many calories are there in an apple?

A 80   B 100   C 120

3 How many calories do you burn if you swim for 20 minutes?

A 60   B 90   C 140

4 How many calories do you burn if you run for 20 minutes?

A 200   B 300   C 400

5 How much water should people drink every day?

A half a litre   B 1 litre   C 2–3 litres

6 How much sleep does an average person get every night?

A 7 hours   B 8.5 hours   C 9.5 hours

5 Pronunciation

▶ CD1 T40 and T41 Turn to page 110.

6 Listen

a ▶ CD1 T42 Match the dishes on the school canteen menu with the pictures. Write the numbers 1–10. Then listen and check.

A

B

C

D

4

E

F

G

H

I

J

Starters
1 Pasta (with tomato sauce)
2 Vegetable soup Ⓥ
3 Mixed salad

Main courses
(with vegetables or chips)
4 Fish
5 Chicken and mushrooms
6 Cheeseburger
7 Vegetarian curry and rice Ⓥ

Desserts
8 Yoghurt (various fruit flavours)
9 Ice cream
10 Cheese

b ▶ CD1 T43 Listen to the dialogue at the school canteen. Write down what Annie and Jack ask for.

1 Annie: _____

2 Jack: _____

7 Grammar

✱ *some* and *any*

a Look at the examples from the dialogue. Complete the rule.

*I'd like **some yoghurt**, please.*
*I'd like **some carrots**.*
*We haven't got **any carrots** today.*
*Do you want **any dessert**?*

> **RULE:** With uncountable and plural nouns, we usually use _____ in positive sentences, and we usually use _____ in negative sentences and questions.

b Complete the sentences with *some* or *any*.

1 I wanted to buy _some_ food, but I didn't have _____ money.

2 A: Have we got _____ homework tonight?
   B: Yes, we've got _____ grammar exercises to do.

3 Mario bought _____ new socks last week, but he didn't buy _____ shoes.

4 A: Let's listen to _____ music.
   B: OK. Did you bring _____ CDs?

5 I'd like to make _____ sandwiches. The problem is I've got _____ cheese, but I haven't got _____ butter.

8 Speak

a In Exercise 6b, who orders a healthy lunch – Annie or Jack? Discuss in a small group.

b Work with a partner. One of you works in the canteen. The other one orders a meal. Then change roles.

Look at the menu in Exercise 6a. Choose what to order.

Use these expressions to help you.

> *What would you like?*   *Can I have … ?*
> *What else?*   *I'd like … , please.*
> *Here you are.*   *Thanks!*

A double ice cream ...

▶ CD1 T44 **Read and listen**

a Look at the photostory. Who do you think orders a double ice cream – Jess or Pete? Read and listen to find the answer.

1

Pete: I really like coming here. It's good after a long day at school.

Jess: Yeah. And today *was* a long day. That lesson this afternoon with Mrs Sanders ... wow!

2

Pete: Didn't you like it?

Jess: It was OK. But, I mean ... how many lessons are we going to have about food and diet and stuff?

Pete: Yeah, I know what you mean. It's important, though.

Jess: Sure, of course it is. But then I look at the cakes and ice cream on this menu and ....

Pete: And?

Jess: There's this little voice inside my head. It's going '*Bad! Bad!*' And it sounds like Mrs Sanders!

3

4

Pete: Yeah, I know that voice.

Jess: I try not to listen to it – but it isn't easy!

Pete: No problem! Order a double ice cream with chocolate sauce.

Jess: Are you serious?

Pete: Absolutely! Look, I know diet is important. But you've got to enjoy life as well.

Jess: That's right. But a double ice cream with chocolate sauce? Isn't that a bit too much?

Pete: Well, yes. That's why I can only do this a couple of times a month!

Jess: Bo-ring!! OK, let's get two!

b Mark the statements *T* (true) or *F* (false).

1 Jess and Pete are at the café after school. [T]
2 They had a lesson today about food. [ ]
3 Jess thinks they have too many lessons about food. [ ]
4 Mrs Sanders says 'Bad! bad!' when Jess looks at the menu. [ ]
5 Pete has a problem with ice cream with chocolate sauce. [ ]
6 Pete is not serious when he says you've got to enjoy life. [ ]
7 Pete only orders double ice cream with chocolate sauce about once a month. [ ]

10 Everyday English

a Find expressions 1–6 in the photostory. Who says them? Match them with the expressions a–f.

1 ... and stuff. `c`

2 I know what you mean. ☐

3 No problem. ☐

4 Absolutely! ☐

5 ... as well. ☐

6 ... a couple of ... ☐

a Yes!

b ... too.

c ... and things like that.

d ... two ...

e It's easy.

f I understand you.

b Read the dialogue. Use the expressions in Exercise 10a to complete it.

Paula: I'm really tired. Too much work!

Julian: [1] _I know what you mean_ . I did three hours of homework last night. French, Maths [2] _____ .

Paula: Me too. But I watched the football on TV [3] _____ .

Julian: Really? So you did your homework after the match? How did you stay awake?

Paula: [4] _____ ! I just drank [5] _____ cups of coffee.

Julian: So, coffee keeps you awake?

Paula: [6] _____ ! I didn't go to sleep for hours. I'm really tired today, though!

> ### Discussion box
> 1 Pete says 'you've got to enjoy life as well'. What do you think?
> 2 How do you relax after a long day at school?

11 Improvisation

Work in groups of three. Take two minutes to prepare a short role play. Try to use some of the expressions from Exercise 10a. Do not write the text, just agree on your ideas for a short scene. Then act it out.

Roles: Pete, Jess and Mrs Sanders

Situation: At the café – a few minutes later

Basic idea: Pete and Jess have just ordered their ice creams. Mrs Sanders has come into the café.

Use one of these sentences to start the conversation:

Mrs Sanders: Jess? Pete? What a surprise to see you here!

Pete: Hello Mrs Sanders. Would you like to join us?

12 Team Spirit ⊙ DVD Episode 3

a How well do you know Jess, Debbie, Pete and Joel? Complete the gaps with their names.

b Watch Episode 3 and check if you were right.

_____ hates gardening.

_____ says _____ eats unhealthily.

_____ thinks he/she isn't overweight.

_____ says that what _____ eats is gross.

_____ wants _____ and _____ to stop arguing.

_____ is worried that the group are not working as a team for the Community Award.

_____ didn't mean to be rude.

13 Write

Write a paragraph about *one* of your partners. Use your notes from Exercise 12 to guide you. Here is an example.

Carol eats three meals a day. She eats a lot of salad and vegetables, but not much meat. She hates carrots! She doesn't eat a lot of snacks but she sometimes has an ice cream or some chocolate. She drinks about two litres of water a day.

Carol thinks it's important to keep fit. She plays basketball once a week. She swims and rides her bike, too, and she enjoys going for walks at the weekend.

14 Last but not least: more speaking

a Read the following questions. Take three minutes to think about your answers. Make notes.

1 Which is your favourite eating place? (a restaurant, a fast food place, your grandma's?) What do you especially like about the place and why? (the food, the people?)

2 Imagine you have your own restaurant. What is it like?
   ● What kind of food and drink do you serve?
   ● Where is it?
   ● What is the style like?
   ● What are the people working there like?
   ● What does it look like?

3 Imagine you are in a restaurant with a famous person.
   ● Who is the person?
   ● Where is the restaurant?
   ● What are you talking about?

b Ask and answer the questions with three other people in your class.

c Share your favourite ideas with the class.

Check your progress

1 Grammar

a Complete the sentences. Use *have/has to* or *don't/doesn't have to.*

1 You ____*have to*____ understand! There is no way I can accept this.

2 If you want to go to university, you _____ study hard.

3 She _____ buy a computer. She can use my laptop.

4 Students at most schools in the UK _____ wear a uniform.

5 I understand what you said. You _____ tell me again!

6 James wants to be healthy. He _____ be careful about what he eats.

7 You _____ help me with my work. I can do it on my own. ☐ **6**

b (Circle) the correct words.

1 She's buying *a / (some)* fruit at the supermarket.

2 Can I have *a / an* orange, please?

3 I can't buy it. I haven't got *much / many* money.

4 How *much / many* tomatoes have we got?

5 *Much / Many* people live in this city.

6 If you want something to eat, have *a / some* sandwich.

7 We've got *a / some* eggs, but we haven't got *much / many* bread.

8 We haven't got *some / any* apples today. Would you like *some / any* carrots?

9 Our teacher never gives us *some / any* homework before the weekend. She's great! ☐ **8**

2 Vocabulary

a Fill in the puzzle with words for food and drink. What's the mystery word?

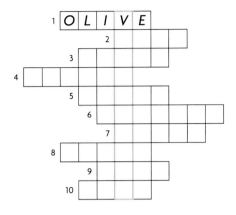

1 ____*Olive*____ oil is a good oil to use in cooking.

2 They come from chickens and you can fry them or boil them _____ .

3 A lot of people put this in coffee.

4 Lots of people drink _____ juice for breakfast.

5 I'd like a glass of mineral _____ .

6 They are orange and they grow under the ground.

7 You need _____ to make toast.

8 A round fruit that is usually red or green.

9 Chicken, lamb and beef, for example.

10 Food that we get from the sea. ☐ **9**

b Put the letters in order to find the names of jobs.

1	cathree	*teacher*	5	lpito	_____
2	tindest	_____	6	wrayel	_____
3	crodot	_____	7	rigefhetifr	_____
4	serun	_____	8	eerening	_____

☐ **7**

How did you do?

Check your score.

Total score	☺	☺	☹
☐ **30**	Very good	OK	Not very good
Grammar	11 – 14	8 – 10	less than 8
Vocabulary	14 – 16	11 –14	less than 11

Learning languages

* Comparatives and superlatives
* Vocabulary: language learning

1 Read and listen

a Look at the pictures and the title of the text. What do you think the text is about? Read the text quickly and check.

b ▶ CD1 T45 Read the text again and listen. Write *T* (true) or *F* (false).

1 Mezzofanti spoke over 38 languages. ☐
2 He travelled to other countries. ☐
3 For Mezzofanti, Arabic was harder to learn than Chinese. ☐
4 One story says that he learned a language in one night. ☐
5 He never met anyone who spoke Old English. ☐

c Do many people in your country speak more than one language? Which languages do people speak?

d One language in the world has more speakers than English. Which do you think it is?

Arabic   Chinese
Russian   Spanish

Speaking in many tongues

Giuseppe Mezzofanti (1774 – 1849) was an Italian Cardinal who was perhaps the best language learner ever. He spoke more than 38 languages fluently. He never left Italy but he learned to speak these languages without an accent. People from all over the world came to talk to him in their mother tongue. All of them were amazed at his fluency.

At the age of 12, Mezzofanti spoke his native Italian, as well as German, Greek, Latin, and at least five other languages. Then he learned Arabic, Russian, Hindi, Old English and Maltese. He also learned Chinese. This was the hardest language for him to learn: it took him four months.

Some stories say he also spoke 30 other languages quite well and that he could understand another 20 (for example, Tibetan and Icelandic.)

Another story says that he heard there were two foreigners in a prison in Rome. So he learned their language in one night and spoke to them the next morning!

It's hard to know if all these stories are true. Some people, for example, ask, 'How did he learn Old English without meeting anyone who spoke it?', or 'Did he really learn a language in a few weeks – or in one night?' We don't know for sure, but we can say for certain that Giuseppe Mezzofanti became a language-learning legend.

2 Listen

▶ CD1 T46 **a** Alessandro and Paula are talking about the languages they are learning. Listen and read.

b ▶ CD1 T46 Listen again and write the names of the languages.

ALESSANDRO (from Italy)
Mother tongue: Italian
Learning: Spanish, German

ALESSANDRO:
My [1] _____ is good – it's better than my [2] _____ . Of course, for me [3] _____ is easier than [4] _____ . That's because it's got a lot of words that are almost the same as [5] _____ . The grammar is very similar, too.

PAULA (from Argentina)
Mother tongue: Spanish
Learning: English, Portuguese

PAULA:
[6] _____ pronunciation is difficult for me. But of course [7] _____ pronunciation is more difficult! I never know how to pronounce a new word, because the writing and the pronunciation are often very different.

3 Grammar

✱ Comparative adjectives

a Underline examples of comparisons in the texts in Exercise 2. Then complete the table.

	Adjectives	Comparative form
short adjectives (one syllable)	long short big	long**er** *shorter* bigg**er**
adjectives ending in -y	easy happy	happi**er** than ...
longer adjectives (two or more syllables)	difficult important	**more** important
irregular adjectives	bad good far	worse _____ further

b Complete the sentences. Choose the correct adjective and use the comparative form.

1 Italian is _more modern than_ (old / modern) Latin.
2 The Amazon River is _____ (short / long) the Nile.
3 Iceland is _____ (big / small) India.
4 For most Europeans, learning Chinese is _____ (easy / difficult) learning Italian.
5 Sydney is _____ (close to / far from) my country _____ Paris.

4 Pronunciation

▶ CD1 T47 Turn to page 110.

5 Speak

Work with a partner. Compare the things in the list. Use adjectives from the box or other adjectives that you know.

> interesting   good
> beautiful   exciting
> friendly   clean   nice
> intelligent   easy
> important   quiet   boring

1 CD-ROMs / books
2 summer / winter
3 football / tennis
4 dogs / cats
5 cities / villages
6 Spanish / German

6 Listen

a ▶ CD1 T48 Listen to the interview with Professor Crystal. <u>Underline</u> the correct answers.

1 The language with the most words is probably English / Chinese / Arabic.

2 Every year, about 250 / 2,500 / 25,000 new words come into English.

3 English has under 1 million / 1 million / more than 1 million words.

4 The most frequent letter in English is a / e / i.

5 There are 5 / 10 / 12 meanings for 'X' in Professor Crystal's book.

b ▶ CD1 T48 Listen again. Answer the questions.

1 How many English words do the two biggest dictionaries list?

2 How many words does a native speaker of English usually have in their active vocabulary?

3 How can a woman who speaks Japanese say 'Yes' when a man asks her to marry him?

4 How can a woman who speaks Igbo say 'Yes' when a man asks her to marry him?

Professor David Crystal is one of the world's most famous experts on language. He is the author of more than 100 books and gives talks all over the world. Two of his most important books are *The Cambridge Encyclopedia of the English Language* and *The Cambridge Encyclopedia of Language*.

7 Vocabulary

✱ Language learning

a Check that you understand these words about learning and speaking languages.

make mistakes   imitate   corrects   translate   look up
~~have an accent~~   means   guess   communicate

b ▶ CD1 T49 Read the text. Fill in the spaces with the words and phrases from Exercise 7a. Then listen and check.

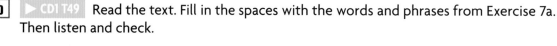

Advice for language learners

" It can sometimes be a little difficult to learn a foreign language fluently. But there are many things you can do to make your learning more successful.

When you speak a foreign language, it's normal to ¹ *have an accent* . That's OK – other people can usually understand. It's a good idea to listen to CDs and try to ² _____ other speakers to make your pronunciation better.

If you see a new word, and you don't know what it ³ _____ , you can sometimes ⁴ _____ the meaning from words you know, or you can ⁵ _____ the word in a dictionary.

A lot of good language learners try not to ⁶ _____ things from their first language. Translation is sometimes a good idea, but try to think in the foreign language if you can!

It's also normal to ⁷ _____ . When your teacher ⁸ _____ a mistake in your writing or speaking, think about it and try to see why it's wrong. But it's more important to ⁹ _____ , so don't be afraid to speak! "

8 Grammar

✳ Superlative adjectives

a Read the sentences on the cards. Two of them are not true. Which do you think they are?

AMAZING FACTS — OR JUST LIES??

> The longest word in the English language is *dispercombobulation* – it has 19 letters.

> The most frequent letter in English is *e*. The least frequent is *q*.

> The easiest language to learn in the world is Portoni, a language spoken in Papua New Guinea. It hasn't got any grammar, and there are only about 1,750 words in the language.

> The shortest place names only have one letter. There are towns in Norway and Sweden called Å and there is a river in Oregon, USA called D.

> There are 820 languages in Papua New Guinea, 742 in Indonesia, and 516 in Nigeria. South Africa has the most official languages in the world.

> Somalia is the only African country where everybody speaks the same language (Somali).

> The longest one-word place name in the world is in New Zealand: *Taumatawhakatangihangakoauauotamateaturipukakapikimaungahoronukupokaiwhenuakitanatahu*

b Cover the text. Can you answer these questions?

1 Which country has the most official languages?
2 What is the most frequent letter in English?
3 In which African country does everyone speak the same language?
4 Which letter is the name of a river in the USA?

c Look at the table. Write the adjectives from the box in the second column. Then fill in the comparative and superlative forms.

difficult   big   happy   fantastic   important

	Adjectives	Comparative form	Superlative form
short adjectives (one syllable)	long short small	longer shorter	the longest ....
short adjectives ending in one vowel + one consonant	.... fat	.... fatter	.... the fattest
adjectives ending in -y	easy	easier	....
longer adjectives (two or more syllables)	frequent	more frequent	the most frequent ....
irregular adjectives	bad good many	worse better more	....

d Complete the sentences. Use the superlative form of the adjectives.

1 Many people say that Hungarian is one of the _most difficult_ (difficult) languages.

2 When Sarah won $1,000, she was the .... (happy) girl in the world.

3 The internet was one of the .... (important) inventions of the 1960s.

4 Vatican City is the .... (small) country in the world.

5 When my grandmother died, it was one of the .... (bad) times in my life.

6 The Amazon is the .... (long) river in the world.

Culture in mind

9 Read and listen

a Think of three words in your own language that teenagers often say, and adults don't say.

b Think of three words in your own language that teachers or parents say a lot, and you never say.

c Share your ideas with a partner.

d ▶ CD2 T1 Read the text and check your ideas.

Teen talk

It's 2010, outside the gates of a school somewhere in the UK. Some teenagers are talking. One says to another, 'I'm tired of jamming after school – it's really vanilla. Let's go for a za, OK?'

Two adults are walking past. They hear what the teenagers are saying, but they don't understand a word. (What the teenager said, was, 'I'm tired of hanging around after school – it's really boring. Let's go for a pizza.')

This is nothing new – teenagers always invent new words and phrases. They create words for everyday things – words that mean, *good* or *parents* or *bad* or *good-looking*, and so on. Look at these different ways of saying *good* in recent decades:

> 1960s – groovy (or fab)
> 1970s – neat
> 1980s – ACE
> 1990s – wicked
> 2000s – cool

But, of course, the words you use depend on your interests, your friends, the music you listen to and the part of the country you live in. Different groups of teenagers have different likes and dislikes, and so they also have different expressions.

So why do teenagers invent new words, or invent new meanings for old words? Many people think it's because they don't want adults to understand, but that probably isn't true – the real reason is that teenagers want to feel that they're part of a group that speaks the same language, a language that is different from the one their parents and other adults speak. And also teenagers like to be creative and play with language, so they have fun creating new words.

And what do *rents* (parents) and *mouldies* (old people) think about it all? Most of them don't worry about it – after all, they had their own special words when they were teenagers too. But, some adults complain about 'teen talk' and get quite annoyed by it. But that's all part of the fun for the teenagers!

e Match the words with their definitions.

1 gates   *f*
2 hang around
3 invent
4 decades
5 expression
6 complain

a to wait or spend time somewhere
b groups of ten years
c a word or a phrase
d to create something new
e to say that something isn't (or wasn't) good
f doors in an outside wall or fence

f Complete the sentences with words from Exercise 9e. Use the correct form when necessary.

1 *Decades* ago, many of the words we use now didn't exist.
2 When I was a child, I loved _____ new words.
3 Some of my friends _____ for hours after school.
4 What does this _____ mean?
5 She _____ to her maths teacher that she had too much homework.
6 Meet me at the park _____ .

10 Write

Do one of these activities.

a Write about the languages you speak. Use the texts by Alessandro and Paula on page 55 to help you.

b Imagine you are doing an English course at a language school in Britain or the USA. Write an email to an English-speaking friend. Think about these questions.

- Where are you writing from? (London, New York, Cambridge?)
- Do you like the English course? What kind of things are you doing in class?
- Who is your teacher?
- How many students are in your class? Where are they from?
- Is your English better now? How? (Is your grammar better? Do you know more words? Do you understand better?)

Start like this:

Dear _____ ,

I'm writing to you from [name of place]. I'm doing an English course here. The course is …

11 Speak

a Read these questions and make notes of your answers.

- What goals do you have for learning English?
  I want to learn 20 new words per week.
  I want to find three interesting texts on the internet per week.
- Why is having better English important for you now?
  I want to be able to understand the words of my favourite songs better.
  I want to be able to watch films in English.
- How difficult/easy is it for you to speak English in class?
- What else can you do to learn English better?
  I can try and speak more English in class.
  I can read more in English.

b Discuss your answers in small groups. Then report to the class.

8 We're going on holiday

* Present continuous for future arrangements
* Vocabulary: future time expressions, holiday activities

1 Read and listen

a Look at this magazine article with ideas for adventure holidays for families. Which of these holidays looks the most interesting? Say why.

b ▶ CD2 T2 Listen to the radio show *Holiday Dreams*. Which of the places do the people go to? Write the numbers in the boxes.

Debbie ☐   Mark ☐

Monica ☐

Family holidays can be fun!

Tour operators are now organising real adventure holidays for families with teens.

1 Camping in Africa in the desert!

Rocks, colours, wildlife – so many things that you can only see here in Africa.

2 Diving in the Red Sea

From the resorts of Egypt's Red Sea coast, you can swim with some of the most beautiful aquatic life in the world.

3 Kayaking in Slovenia

Join us in Slovenia as we race down the River Soča!

4 Volunteering

There's lots of volunteer work to choose from. How about helping conserve the elephant population of Thailand?

5 Seeing the delights of a winter wonderland

The cold weather doesn't worry you? Then come and have fun with a dog team pulling you across the snow!

c ▶ CD2 T3 Listen to Sara talking to her friend, Anna, about her holiday plans. Complete the dialogue with the correct present continuous forms.

Sara: Hey, Anna! How's your day going?

Anna: Good! My mum and I are planning the family holiday.

Sara: Excellent! Where are you going?

Anna: Well, listen to this! We're [1] _____ to Thailand!

Sara: Wow! Really? When?

Anna: In two months' time. We're [2] _____ on 8 May.

Sara: How are you getting there?

Anna: First we're [3] _____ to Bangkok.

Sara: Oh. And are you [4] _____ in Bangkok?

Anna: Oh no! We're [5] _____ on to Chang Mai. And … this is the best bit! We're [6] _____ some work at the elephant conservation centre!

Sara: Amazing! What are you [7] _____ there?

Anna: We're [8] _____ after the elephants. We're [9] _____ things like washing them and cleaning their feet.

Sara: It sounds brilliant! Are all your family [10] _____ with you?

Anna: Yes! But it's a bit expensive. Dad almost fainted when he heard how much we're paying.

2 Grammar

✱ Present continuous for future arrangements

a <u>Underline</u> other examples of the present continuous in the dialogue in Exercise 1c.

We're going to Thailand.
We're leaving on 8 May.

> **RULE:** We often use the present continuous to talk about plans and arrangements for the future.

b Complete the sentences.

Use the present continuous form of the verbs.

1 I *'m visiting* (visit) my grandparents in Rome next year.

2 Come to our place next Saturday. We _____ (have) a party.

3 Mum _____ (take) my sister to London on Thursday. They _____ (leave) early in the morning.

4 A: _____ you _____ (go) out tonight?
   B: No, I _____ (stay) at home.

5 My brother _____ (not come) on holiday with us this year. He _____ (work) in a shop for six weeks.

6 I've got toothache, so I _____ (see) the dentist tomorrow.

3 Vocabulary

✱ Future time expressions

a Here are some expressions we can use to talk about the future. How do you say them in your language?

> tomorrow
> next week/Saturday/month/weekend
> in two/five days' time
> the day after tomorrow
> the week after next
> on Saturday morning/Sunday afternoon

b Answer the questions.

1 What day is the day after tomorrow?

2 What day is it in three days' time?

3 How many days is it until next Sunday?

4 What month is the month after next?

4 Speak

a Tell a partner what you're doing:

● this evening
● on Sunday morning
● next summer

b Now work with another partner. Tell him/her what you and your friend are doing.

A: *This evening I'm staying at home to watch my new DVD.*

B: *My friend is going to the internet café on Sunday morning.*

5 Read

a What do you know about South Africa? Read the questions and (circle) your answers. If you don't know the answers, guess them.

1 What is the capital of South Africa?
   a Cape Town   b Pretoria   c Johannesburg

2 What's the population of Cape Town?
   a about 3,500,000   b about 2,000,000
   c about 10,000,000

3 How many tourists visit Cape Town every year?
   a about 1,000,000   b about 5,000,000
   c about 2,000,000

4 What might you see at Boulders Beach?
   a shipwrecks   b penguins   c sharks

b Now read the text and check your answers to the questions in Exercise 5a.

c Find an adjective in the text to describe these things.

the beaches: ....

the shopping: ....

the settings: ....

the climate: ....

Welcome to Cape Town – the city that has everything!

About two million tourists visit Cape Town every year. It isn't the capital city (that's Pretoria) and it isn't the biggest city either (that's Johannesburg), but Cape Town is South Africa's most popular city with tourists for its many attractions, sights and activities. From the beautiful scenery and sunny beaches to great shopping in the city centre, Cape Town has something for everyone. In fact, a holiday in Cape Town is unforgettable!

Adventure & Outdoors

For the adventure, outdoor or sports fan Cape Town has a range of activities from hiking, climbing and parachuting to diving and golf – all combined with fantastic settings and sunny skies.

Watersports & Diving

Cape Town's beaches are ideal for water sports, including surfing, windsurfing and kayaking. Scuba diving is also popular: the many shipwrecks along the coastline offer some excellent dives. The more adventurous diver can even try shark cage diving to get eye-to-eye with a great white!

If you aren't so adventurous, try a visit to Boulders Beach. It's part of a conservation area for the African penguin. You can walk around on wooden paths and watch the penguins in their natural habitat. It's great for swimming and exploring too – if you don't mind coming face-to-face with a penguin or two!

A few Facts & Figures

Cape Town's climate is pleasant. In summer it's about 26 °C (and remember, mid-summer here is January!) and the winter temperatures don't usually fall below 10 °C. The local currency is the rand; there are one hundred cents to every rand. The three main languages are Xhosa, English and Afrikaans. The population of Cape Town is about 3.5 million.

6 Vocabulary

✱ Holiday activities

a ▶ CD2 T4 Write the names of the activities under the pictures. Then listen, check and repeat.

hiking   climbing   parachuting   scuba diving   golf   surfing   windsurfing   kayaking
canoeing   snorkelling   ~~sailing~~   camping   sightseeing   sunbathing   horse riding

A

.... *sailing* ....

B

....

C

....

D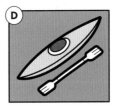

....

E

....

F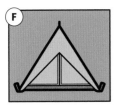

....

G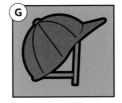

....

H

....

I

....

J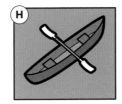

....

K

....

L

....

M

....

N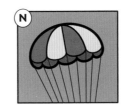

....

O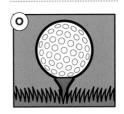

....

b Work with a partner. Which of the activities do you like doing on holiday?

A: *I like windsurfing, but I'm not very good at it.*

B: *I don't like sunbathing. It's boring.*

c Fill in each space with a verb from the box.

hire   travel   stay   ~~buy~~   spend

1 ___*buy*___ souvenirs / presents / postcards / stamps

2 .... in a hotel / in a bed and breakfast / at a campsite / in a youth hostel / at home

3 .... to Ireland / by ferry / by car / by plane / by train / by coach

4 .... your holidays (in South Africa) / some time (on the beach) / two weeks (in Greece)

5 .... a car / a boat / a bike / a surfboard

Vocabulary bank Turn to page 115.

7 Speak

a Make a list of all the different kinds of holidays and holiday places in this unit.

b Imagine your family is planning a holiday. Look at your list and choose a place to visit.

c Make notes about your holiday plans:
- Where are you going?
- How long are you staying and where are you staying?
- What are you planning to do there?
- How are you getting there?

d Work with a partner. Ask and answer questions.

A: *Where are you going for your next holiday?*

B: *We're going to …*

8 Pronunciation

▶ CD2 T5 and T6 Turn to page 111.

Having fun?

9 ▶ CD2 T7 **Read and listen**

a Look at the photostory. Where are they? How do they feel in the first photograph? How do they feel in the last photograph? Who does Debbie talk to? Read and listen to find the answers.

Joel: This is no fun at all.

Jess: I'm not enjoying myself.

Pete: You're not the only one.

Debbie: Hang on – I've got a call.

Debbie: Oh hi Dad! Yeah, fine thanks. Sorry? No, we're all having a really good time! No, don't worry. It's raining a bit, but we're having lots of fun. OK. Bye!

Joel: Debbie – are you mad?

Pete: Us? Having fun? In this rain?

Jess: I can't believe you said that!

Debbie: Look, there's no way I'm telling my dad that we're having a bad time. And I'm not going to tell people at school, either. And anyway – if we aren't having fun, it's our fault, isn't it?

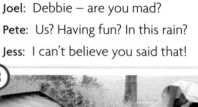

Pete: Let's play a game, then.

Jess: Or sing a song.

Joel: Or we could have a swimming competition!

Jess: Ah, Joel!

Debbie: See? Now we really *are* having a good time!

b Match the beginnings and endings to make a summary of the story.

1	Joel, Jess, Pete and Debbie	a calls Debbie.
2	Debbie's Dad	b to know that they aren't having a good time.
3	Debbie tells her dad that they	c having a good time.
4	Joel, Pete and Jess	d aren't enjoying themselves.
5	Debbie doesn't want people	e are having a good time.
6	In the end, they all start	f are very surprised by what Debbie says.

10 Everyday English

a Find expressions 1–6 in the photostory. Who says them? How do you say the underlined parts in your language?

1 This is no fun <u>at all</u>.

2 <u>Hang on</u>.

3 No, <u>don't worry</u>.

4 I'm not going to tell people at school, <u>either</u>.

5 <u>it's</u> our <u>fault</u>

6 Let's play a game, <u>then</u>.

b Read the dialogue. Use the underlined parts of the expressions in Exercise 10a to complete it.

Sam: Let's go shopping. There's a great new music shop in town.

Louise: I can't. I haven't got any money ¹ _at all_ .

Sam: Well, ask your parents for some money, ² _____ .

Louise: I can't. They gave me some money yesterday. I spent it all last night, though.

Sam: OK – so ³ _____ your _____ that you haven't got any money.

Louise: Absolutely. ⁴ _____ – perhaps I can ask my grandparents.

Sam: Good idea.

Louise: No – I can't ask them, ⁵ _____ . They're in France on holiday.

Sam: OK – ⁶ _____ . I'll go shopping alone. No problem!

Discussion box

1 Debbie says: 'If we aren't having fun, it's our fault, isn't it?' What is your opinion about this?

2 How does the weather influence <u>your</u> feelings? Give examples.

3 Think of a situation that wasn't very nice but you still had fun. Say what happened.

11 Improvisation

Work with a partner. Take two minutes to prepare a short role play. Try to use some of the expressions from Exercise 10a. Do not write the text, just agree on your ideas for a short scene. Then act it out.

Roles: Pete and Joel

Situation: At Pete's place – a week later

Basic idea: Pete and Joel want to play football, but they can't because it's raining a lot.

Use one of these sentences to start the conversation:

Pete: I can't believe it. We want to play football and it's raining.

Joel: Hey, I think this is great!

12 Team Spirit ⊙ DVD Episode 4

a Imagine you are going on a camping trip. Look at these things and put them in order of importance 1–10. (1 = very important / 10 = not important). Then discuss in small groups. Explain your reasons for each object.

mineral water

MP3 player

boots

baked beans

mobile

camping trip

plates and cutlery

favourite piece of clothing

book

tin opener

matches

b Watch Episode 4 and find out about Jess, Debbie, Joel and Pete's camping trip.

13 Write

a Imagine you got this email from your friend, Cynthia. How does she feel? Why?

Hi … (your name),

I'm so excited. Guess what – it's my Dad's 40th birthday next month, and so he's taking us all to London for a weekend! Cool, eh?

We're flying over on the Thursday evening. As soon as we arrive, we're going on a tour of the city. They say London is really beautiful by night, and I'm really looking forward to seeing all those famous places.

On the Friday we're going to the Tate Modern (the art gallery near the river Thames), then to the Design Museum. It's not far from our hotel, so we're planning to walk there. In the afternoon, we're going on the London Eye. I can't wait to see the Houses of Parliament from up there!

Saturday is for shopping – there's no doubt about that! We're going to Portobello Road first. Then in the afternoon, we're visiting Harrods – the most famous shop in London! Dad's not very happy about it, but I'm sure he'll enjoy it when we're there.

On Sunday morning we're going to Hyde Park, and we're flying home in the afternoon. It's my dream trip – and it's happening!

Hope everything's OK with you.

Love, Cynthia

---

b Write back to Cynthia. In your email, tell her about a trip you are going on. Include this information about the arrangement:

- where and when you are going
- who you are going with
- how you are travelling
- where you are staying
- what you are doing there
- how long you are staying

14 Last but not least: more speaking

Work with a partner.

Student A: Look at the card below.

Student B: Turn to page 126.

Ask questions to find out when and where your partner is going on holiday and what they are going to do there.

Student A:

Destination: Australia

Dates: 8 November – 6 December

Travel arrangements: fly from London Heathrow to Sydney (Kingsford Smith) International Airport

Hotel: Hilton Sydney

Trips: Sydney Harbour Cruise, Blue Mountain Tour

Activities: surfing off Bondi Beach

Check your progress

1 Grammar

a Complete the sentences. Use the comparative or superlative form of the adjectives.

1 Today is the ___longest___ (long) day of the year.

2 For me, Geography is _____ (difficult) than Maths. It's difficult for me to remember facts about countries.

3 History is the _____ (easy) subject at school.

4 I feel dreadful! This is the _____ (bad) day of my life!

5 I don't argue with Joe, because he's _____ (big) than me.

6 Sally is _____ (good) than me at Art.

7 I think my results will be _____ (bad) this year than last year.

8 If you want to be fit, a healthy diet and lots of exercise are the _____ (important) things.

[7]

b Look at Linda's diary. Write sentences about the things she's doing next weekend.

> **Saturday**
> 10.00 driving lesson
> 3.00 meet Gerard in café
> 6.00 cinema with Sue
> **Sunday**
> 12.30 lunch with Wendy
> 5.00 homework
> 7.30 cousins arrive from Canada!

Saturday

1 At 10.00 she _'s having a driving lesson._

2 At 3.00 she _____ .

3 At 6.00 she and Sue _____ .

Sunday

4 At 12.30 she and Wendy _____ .

5 At 5.00 _____ .

6 At 7.30 _____ .

[5]

2 Vocabulary

a Complete the sentences with the words in the box.

> imitate   translate   ~~make mistakes~~
> look up   accent   mean   guess
> communicate

1 When I speak English, I sometimes ___make mistakes___ in grammar, but I can still _____ with English speakers.

2 Excuse me, what does this word _____ ?

3 I want my pronunciation to be better, so I listen to cassettes and _____ the speakers.

4 For homework, our teacher sometimes gives us texts in English and we have to _____ them into our language.

5 My father speaks good English, but he has a very strong _____ .

6 When I don't know a word, I try to _____ the meaning. If I can't do that, I _____ the word in my dictionary.

[7]

b Write the holiday activities in the lists.

> climbing   windsurfing   ~~swimming~~
> camping   horse riding   sightseeing
> snorkelling   canoeing   surfing
> sunbathing

in/on water	not in/on water
swimming	_____
_____	_____
_____	_____
_____	_____
_____	_____

[9]

How did you do?

Check your score.

Total score	😊	😐	😞
[28]	Very good	OK	Not very good
Grammar	11 – 12	9 – 10	less than 9
Vocabulary	13 – 16	10 –12	less than 10

9 It'll never happen

* *will/won't*
* Vocabulary: expressions to talk about the future, expressions to talk about fortune telling

1 Read and listen

a ▶ CD2 T8 Look at the predictions for the future. Match the predictions with the people in the pictures. Then listen and check your answers.

1 'I think they'll have special machines that do X-rays of cars so that when they break down, we can find out immediately what's wrong with them.'

2 'I reckon that one day we'll be able to totally control the weather. We won't have any more bad storms and hurricanes any more.'

3 'One day, there won't be any real toys any more. Kids will play with virtual toys. I think that'll be very sad.'

4 'I'm sure one day scientists will invent little robots that are so cheap we can all afford to buy one and keep it at home to help in the house and stuff.'

5 'In the future, there will be some great inventions. I bet very rich people will have their own personal space rockets so they can fly off into space whenever they feel like it!'

b Read the predictions again. Mark them: (1) I totally believe this will happen / (2) I'm not sure this will happen / (3) This won't happen. Now compare your views with other students.

Getting the future wrong!

People love reading predictions. They love looking into the future. They want to know what will or won't happen – tomorrow, next week, next year, in the next century.

But predictions are not always right – they can go very, very wrong! Here are some of our favourite 'predictions that went wrong'.

* In 1859, a man called Edwin Drake wanted to drill for oil. A worker said, 'Drill for oil? You mean make a hole in the ground to find oil? You're crazy. It won't work.'

* In 1872, the US President Rutherford B. Hayes, looked at Alexander Bell's new telephone and said, 'It's a great invention, but who will want to use it?'

* In 1899, a top British scientist said, 'Radio has no future, and X-rays won't work.'

* In 1908, a French general said, 'Aeroplanes are interesting toys – but they'll never be important for war.'

c Now read the text. Did you know about any of these predictions that went wrong? Which is your favourite prediction?

d ▶ CD2 T9 Read the text again and listen. Complete the sentences to express what people said.

1 The boss of a big film company said, 'There will never be …'

2 The boss of a record company said, 'The Beatles …'.

3 The boss of a big computer company said, 'Not many people …'.

4 A US President said about the telephone, 'Not many people …'.

e Discuss in class.

Write three predictions for the future – two you believe will happen and one crazy one. Don't tell your partner which is the one you don't believe will happen. Read them out to each other and try to guess which is the 'crazy' one.

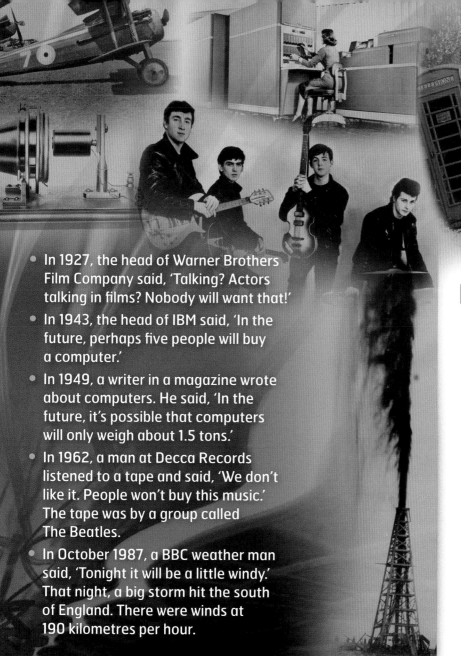

- In 1927, the head of Warner Brothers Film Company said, 'Talking? Actors talking in films? Nobody will want that!'
- In 1943, the head of IBM said, 'In the future, perhaps five people will buy a computer.'
- In 1949, a writer in a magazine wrote about computers. He said, 'In the future, it's possible that computers will only weigh about 1.5 tons.'
- In 1962, a man at Decca Records listened to a tape and said, 'We don't like it. People won't buy this music.' The tape was by a group called The Beatles.
- In October 1987, a BBC weather man said, 'Tonight it will be a little windy.' That night, a big storm hit the south of England. There were winds at 190 kilometres per hour.

2 Grammar

✱ *will/won't*

a Look at the examples. <u>Underline</u> examples of *will/'ll* and *won't* in the texts in Exercise 1.

I think they'll have special machines.
Five people will buy a computer.   It won't work.

b Complete the table and the rule.

Positive	Negative	Question	Short answers
I/you/we/ they/he/she/ it .... (**will**) come	I/you/we/ they/he/she/ it .... (**will not**) come	.... I/you/ we/they/he/ she/it come?	Yes, I/you/we/they/ he/she/it .... No, I/you/we/they/he/ .... she/it (**will not**).

RULE: We use .... (*will*) or .... (*will not*) + base form to make predictions about the future.

c Complete the dialogue with *'ll*, *will* or *won't* and a verb from the box.

> stay   go   find   give
> be   ~~get~~   help

Clara: Oh, Pete, it's the maths test tomorrow! I hate Maths. I'm sure I ¹ *won't get* the answers right!

Pete: Don't worry, you ² .... fine! You got a good result in your last test.

Clara: Yes, but this is more difficult. I really don't feel well. Maybe I ³ .... to school tomorrow. I ⁴ .... in bed all day.

Pete: That ⁵ .... you. The teacher ⁶ .... you the test on Wednesday.

Clara: You're right. But what can I do?

Pete: Look, why don't I come round to your place this afternoon after school? We can look at the Maths together. You ⁷ .... it's not so difficult.

Clara: Oh, thanks, Pete.

d Work with a partner. Act out the dialogue in Exercise 2c.

3 Pronunciation

 CD2 T10   Turn to page 111.

4 Listen

▶ CD2 T11 Listen to Sally and Patrick talking about the future, and complete the first two columns of the table. Tick (✓) the things they think will happen and cross (✗) the things they think won't happen.

	Sally	Patrick	Me	My partner
get married	✓			
have children				
go to university				
get a good job				
learn to drive				
become famous				

5 Vocabulary

✱ Expressions to talk about the future

a Sally says, 'I hope to get a good job.' Does she want to get a good job? Is she sure she'll get one? How do you say, 'I hope to' in your language?

b Look at these sentences from the dialogue. Write the underlined phrases in the correct column.

1 I think I'll get married.
2 I'll probably go to university.
3 I don't think I'll live abroad.
4 I doubt I'll be famous.

5 Maybe I'll get married.
6 I'm sure I won't have children.
7 I hope to get a good job.
8 I'm sure I'll learn to drive.

A I believe this will happen	B I believe this won't happen	C I think it's possible that this will happen
I think I'll ...		

6 Speak

a Look at the table in Exercise 4. Complete the *Me* column with your own answers.

b Work with a partner. Guess what your partner's answer will be to the questions. Then ask him/her the questions and complete the *My partner* column of the table.

A: *Will you get married and have children?*   B: *Yes, I'll probably get married and I hope to have children.*

c Compare your answers with other students.

Listen: a song

a  Listen to the song.

When I'm Sixty-four
The Beatles

If I'd been out till quarter to three,
Would you lock the door?
Will you still need me, will you still feed me,
When I'm sixty-four?

You'll be older too,
And if you say the word,
I could stay with you.

I could be handy, mending a fuse
When your lights have gone.
You can knit a sweater by the fireside,
Sunday morning go for a ride.

Doing the garden, digging the weeds,
Who could ask for more?
Will you still need me, will you still feed me,
When I'm sixty-four?

Every summer we can rent a cottage
In the Isle of Wight, if it's not too dear.
We shall scrimp and save.
Grandchildren on your knee,
Vera, Chuck and Dave.

Send me a postcard, drop me a line,
Stating point of view.
Indicate precisely what you mean to say,
Yours sincerely, wasting away.

Give me your answer, fill in a form,
Mine for evermore.
Will you still need me, will you still feed me,
When I'm sixty-four?

b Match the words with their definitions.

1 lock — *i*
2 feed
3 handy
4 mend a fuse
5 dig the weeds
6 cottage
7 scrimp and save
8 drop me a line
9 waste away
10 fill in a form

a try hard to save money
b repair something electrical
c take out plants you don't want in the garden
d a small house in the country
e give food to
f write to me
g useful, practical
h write down official information
i close with a key
j get very thin because you're ill or don't eat

c Listen to the song again and choose the best answer for the questions.

1 What is the singer trying to do in the song?
   a Get a gardening job.
   b Tell his wife to spend less money.
   c Ask someone to marry him.
   d Ask for food.

2 The singer
   a thinks his wife is angry with him.
   b imagines their future life together.
   c has three grandchildren.
   d wants to know if his girlfriend can cook and knit.

3 The singer imagines that their future will be
   a simple and modest.
   b busy.
   c hard work.
   d one long holiday.

d Play the song again and sing along.

Culture in mind

8 Read and listen

a Work in small groups.

Think of methods that people use to try and predict the future. Use the pictures on the page to help you.

b ▶ CD2 T13 Read the text and answer.

Which method of fortune telling:

1 uses part of your hand?
2 looks at when a person was born?
3 includes numbers?
4 uses a drink?
5 can give information about your health?
6 is new?
7 is in newspapers or magazines?
8 is the oldest?

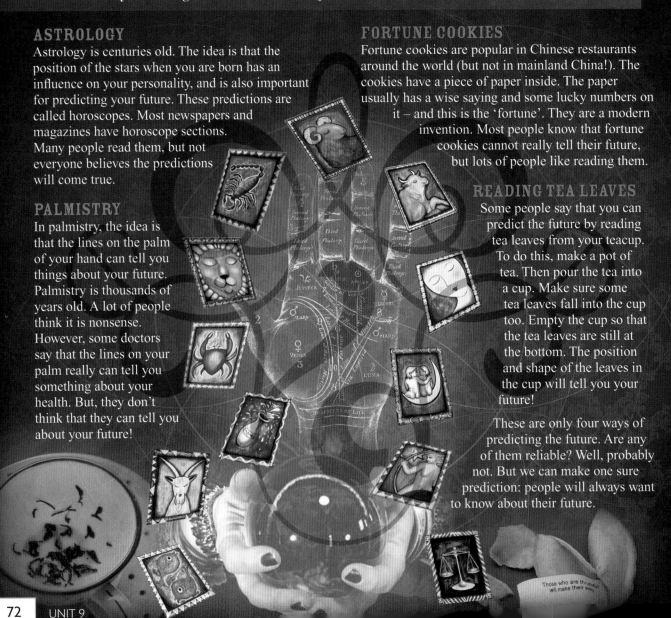

FORTUNE TELLING

Everyone wants to know the answer to questions like: Will I have a lot of money? Will I be happy and healthy? That's why fortune telling is so popular. There are hundreds of different ways of telling the future – here are just a few.

ASTROLOGY

Astrology is centuries old. The idea is that the position of the stars when you are born has an influence on your personality, and is also important for predicting your future. These predictions are called horoscopes. Most newspapers and magazines have horoscope sections. Many people read them, but not everyone believes the predictions will come true.

PALMISTRY

In palmistry, the idea is that the lines on the palm of your hand can tell you things about your future. Palmistry is thousands of years old. A lot of people think it is nonsense. However, some doctors say that the lines on your palm really can tell you something about your health. But, they don't think that they can tell you about your future!

FORTUNE COOKIES

Fortune cookies are popular in Chinese restaurants around the world (but not in mainland China!). The cookies have a piece of paper inside. The paper usually has a wise saying and some lucky numbers on it – and this is the 'fortune'. They are a modern invention. Most people know that fortune cookies cannot really tell their future, but lots of people like reading them.

READING TEA LEAVES

Some people say that you can predict the future by reading tea leaves from your teacup. To do this, make a pot of tea. Then pour the tea into a cup. Make sure some tea leaves fall into the cup too. Empty the cup so that the tea leaves are still at the bottom. The position and shape of the leaves in the cup will tell you your future!

These are only four ways of predicting the future. Are any of them reliable? Well, probably not. But we can make one sure prediction: people will always want to know about their future.

9 Vocabulary

✳ Expressions to talk about fortune telling

a (Circle) the correct definition for each of these words from the text.

1 fortune telling
   a reading science fiction books and watching science fiction films
   (b) saying what will happen in the future

2 century
   a a thousand years
   b a hundred years

3 influence
   a the information your friends give you
   b the power to have an effect on people or things

4 to predict
   a to ask someone what will happen
   b to say what you think will happen

5 palm
   a the inner part of one's hand
   b the outer part of one's hand

6 nonsense
   a something that is unusual
   b something that does not have meaning

7 leaves
   a the green parts of a tree or plant
   b bags of tea

8 reliable
   a if someone is reliable you can trust them
   b if someone is reliable you can't trust them

b Use words in Exercise 9a to complete these sentences. Remember you may need to change the form of the words.

1 I think all these ways of _fortune telling_ are just _____ .

2 If you study a lot, it will have a big _____ on your exam results.

3 I guess life was very different a few _____ ago.

4 My new MP3 player is really small – I can put it in the _____ of my hand.

5 I don't think that the _____ in my teacup can _____ my future.

6 Aaron says he'll do something but he never does it! He's not _____ .

10 Write

a Read this student's predictions about life in the future. Complete the text with words from the box.

will be   ~~be like~~   won't be   will happen
They'll do   will learn   we'll recycle   will find

What will life [1] ___be like___ one hundred years from now? I don't know, of course. But this is what I think [2] _____ .

First, I think that computers [3] _____ much more important in our lives. There [4] _____ any televisions or DVD players or things like that. I think all those things will be part of a computer. And everything in our house will be controlled by computers. I believe scientists [5] _____ a way to make computers talk and think, just like people. That's scary!

Also there won't be any more pollution. Governments will find ways to stop pollution and [6] _____ everything.

Finally, I think that there won't be any schools. Some people say teachers will be robots in the future but I don't think that's true. I think kids [7] _____ at home, using their computers. [8] _____ everything online. (Great, because when they're bored, they can have a bit of fun and play a few online games!)

That's what I think about life in the future. I think it'll be very different, but very exciting!

b Now write your own text (150 words), with the title:

What will life be like two hundred years from now?

11 Speak

a Work with a partner. Talk about the methods of fortune telling in the text on page 72. Discuss these questions:

● What do you think of each method?

● What other methods of fortune telling do you know of?

b Invent a new method of fortune telling! It can be as scientific or crazy as you like!

For your portfolio

Don't give up

* _too_ + adjective, adverbs
* Vocabulary: the weather

1 Read and listen

a Look at the pictures. What do they show?

b Read the text quickly to find out why the river was important to Juliane.

JUNGLE SURVIVAL

On 24 December, 1971, 17-year-old Juliane Köpcke got on a plane with her mother in Lima, Peru, to fly to another city to meet her father.

Over the Amazon jungle, there was a thunderstorm. The rain fell heavily and there was a strong wind. And then lightning hit the plane at 3,000 metres, and it exploded. Juliane fell quickly through the air in her seat and hit the trees hard. For three hours, she was unconscious. When she woke up, her right arm was cut, her shoulder hurt badly and she couldn't see in one eye. She was alone. But she was alive!

Map showing Peru, with Pucallpa and Lima marked.

Juliane's father was a biologist and when she was small, he taught her how to survive in the jungle. She found a small river and walked slowly along it. 'If I follow the river,' she thought, 'I'll find people.' The river also gave her clean water to drink. It was extremely hot, but the river water kept her cool. Sometimes she had to swim in the river because it was too deep to walk in. There were crocodiles in the water but they didn't attack her! There was fruit on some trees but she didn't eat it – she knew it was too dangerous.

Juliane walked for ten days. At night she stopped to sleep because it was too dark to walk. Ten days after the crash, she found a small hut by the river. There were some woodcutters in the hut. They cleaned her cuts carefully and the next day, they carried her down the river, and a plane took her safely back to the city of Pucallpa.

Juliane was the only person who survived the plane crash. The other 91 people, including her mother, all died.

The film director, Werner Herzog, had a ticket to travel on the plane but missed it. Thirty years later, he made a documentary film called 'Wings of Hope' about Juliane and her incredible story.

c The title of the text is 'Jungle survival'. Work with a partner and talk about the difficulties of surviving in the jungle.

Juliane Köpcke in April 1972

d [▶ CD2.T14] Now read the text again and listen. Complete the sentences with words from the text.

1   Rain can fall h＿＿＿＿ .
2   Juliane fell through the air q＿＿＿＿ .
3   She walked s＿＿＿＿ along the river.
4   If you arrive somewhere without any problems, you arrive s＿＿＿＿ .

e Discuss in class.

1   Would you like to see the film *Wings of Hope*? Why/why not?
2   Why do you think Werner Herzog decided to make a film about the plane crash?

② Grammar

✱ *too* + adjective

a Match the two parts of the sentences. How do you say the underlined words in your language?

1   There was fruit on some trees but she didn't eat it –
2   At night she stopped to sleep because
3   She swam in the river because

a   the water was <u>too deep</u> to walk in.
b   she knew it was <u>too dangerous</u>.
c   it was <u>too dark</u> to walk.

b Complete the sentences with *too* and an adjective.

1   I can't watch the rest of the film. I'm *too tired* ! So I'm going to bed.
2   It's ＿＿＿＿ to go swimming today. We'll freeze!
3   Grandma doesn't want to come to the party. She says she's ＿＿＿＿ for parties and dancing!
4   I want a new mobile phone but they're ＿＿＿＿ . I don't have that much money.
5   I didn't like the film – it was ＿＿＿＿ . I only like short films.
6   He didn't answer any of the questions. They were all ＿＿＿＿ .

c Complete the sentences. Use *too* or *very* and a word from the box.

old   big   heavy

1   Look at that house. It's ＿＿＿＿ .

2   I think this hat is ＿＿＿＿ .

3   I can't lift it. It's ＿＿＿＿ .

4   These bags are ＿＿＿＿ .

5   These paintings are ＿＿＿＿ .

6   We can't use this phone now. It's ＿＿＿＿ .

3 Vocabulary

✱ The weather

a Complete the sentences with the words in the box.

> sun   thunder   lightning
> hot   shower   ~~wind~~

1 It was a very cold day and the ___wind___ was really cold too.

2 _____ hit that tree six months ago.

3 Don't sit out in the _____ for too long; you'll burn.

4 Gosh! What was that noise? I think it was _____ .

5 It's much too _____ to go for a walk at the moment.

6 It didn't rain heavily – it was just a _____ , really.

b ▶ CD2 T15 **Listen and complete the weather forecast.**

And now for today's forecast. In the London area, the weather will be [1] ___warm___ with temperatures of around 18 °C. Although the sun will shine for a while, we can expect some strong [2] _____ this afternoon. And that will make it feel quite cool.

Further north in the Birmingham area, things won't be too good, I'm afraid. After last night's [3] _____ , Birmingham is going to be very [4] _____ with an expected high of about 14 °C. But no more [5] _____ and [6] _____ today, at least. And finally, in Scotland, it will be [7] _____ for part of the morning then [8] _____ later on. But not snowing like it was yesterday, fortunately, so the roads should be safer once the fog clears.

c Write three sentences to describe what the weather will be like tomorrow where you are. Compare your predictions with a partner and check tomorrow.

Vocabulary bank Turn to page 115.

4 Grammar

✱ Adverbs

a Look at the examples from the text on page 74 and complete the rule.

*The rain fell **heavily**.*
*It was **extremely** hot.*
*A plane took her **safely** back to the city of Pucallpa.*

> **RULE:** Adverbs describe adjectives and _____
> To form a regular adverb, we usually add _____ to the adjective. If the adjective ends with y, change the y to _____ before adding _____ .

b Underline more examples of adverbs in the text on page 74.

c Complete the tables.

Adjectives	Regular adverbs
slow	_slowly_
bad	_____
loud	_____
quiet	_____
lucky	_____
easy	_____

Adjectives	Irregular adverbs
fast	_fast_
good	_____
early	_early_
late	_late_
hard	_____

d Complete the sentences. Use adverbs from the tables in Exercise 4c.

1 I play the piano ___badly___ , but I can sing quite _____ .

2 She talks very _____ . It's often difficult to hear her.

3 They missed the train because they arrived _____ .

4 If you want to pass your exam, you need to study _____ .

5 Speak

a Work with a partner. Ask and answer the questions.

1 Do you study better early or late in the day?

2 Do you prefer to walk quickly or slowly?

3 Do you play your music loudly or quietly?

4 Do you do your homework slowly or quickly?

b Tell your partner about other things you do. Use the adverbs in the box.

fast   slowly   well   badly   loudly   carefully   lazily   impatiently

A: *I can speak French quite well.*

B: *I do most of my homework well but I do Maths badly.*

6 Pronunciation

▶ CD2 T16 and T17   Turn to page 111.

7 Listen and speak

a Look at the pictures of Hermann Maier. Work with a partner and put the pictures in order. Then tell the story of Hermann Maier's life together.

A

B

C

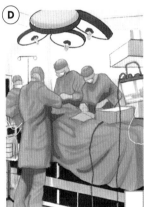
D

E

F

G

b ▶ CD2 T18   Listen to a boy and his father talking about Hermann Maier. Check your version of the story.

c ▶ CD2 T18   Listen again and match the two parts of the sentences.

1 When Hermann was 15,   a Hermann got into the Austrian skiing team.
2 For a time,   b a car hit him.
3 In 1996,   c he was sent home from skiing school.
4 In 1998,   d he won the World Cup!
5 In 2001,   e Hermann worked as a bricklayer.
6 In 2004,   f Hermann won an Olympic Gold medal.

d Work with a partner. Take it in turns to be Hermann Maier. Tell each other your life story. Use your own words and try to describe your (Hermann's) feelings.

Keep on running

 8 ► CD2 T19 **Read and listen**

a Look at the photostory. What are Jess and Joel doing? Why isn't Jess very happy? What does Joel tell her to do? Read and listen to find the answers.

1

Joel: This is OK. In fact, it's good fun!

Jess: Yeah. It's not bad.

Joel: Are you OK, Jess?

2

Jess: Well, no, not really. I've got this pain, right here. Near my stomach.

Joel: Oh dear.

Jess: Yeah, it really hurts. I'm going to stop.

Joel: No. You have to keep on running. And press with your hand, right where it hurts. But whatever you do – don't stop!

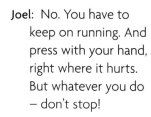

3

4

Jess: Keep on running? Are you sure?

Joel: Yeah. I know it sounds weird, in a way ... but it's the best thing to do.

5

Jess: Well, Joel, you were right. The pain's gone!

Joel: See? Just keep going! But ... Jess, maybe we could stop in a minute? I'm a bit tired now!

Jess: Ah, Joel – don't be such a wimp!

b There is something wrong in each sentence. Cross through the incorrect information and change it.

1 Joel thinks running is ~~horrible~~. ___*good fun*___

2 Jess has got a pain near her neck. _____

3 Jess is going to cry. _____

4 Joel says that Jess has to stop running. _____

5 Joel says that not stopping is the wrong thing to do. _____

6 Jess's pain doesn't go away. _____

7 Joel wants to stop running now. _____

9 Everyday English

a Find expressions 1–6 in the photostory. Who says them? How do you say them in your language?

1 In fact, …
2 Not really.
3 Are you sure?
4 … in a way …
5 … the best thing to do.
6 … in a minute?

b Read the dialogues. Use the expressions in Exercise 9a to complete them.

1 A: James? Can you come and help me?

   B: _In a minute_ . I'm working.

2 A: I've got a terrible headache.

   B: Well, take an aspirin and go to bed. That's _____ .

3 A: This record is by The Beatles.

   B: _____ ? I think it's The Rolling Stones.

4 A: Would you like to watch a DVD with me?

   B: No, _____ , thanks. I've got to do some work.

5 A: This is a great film.

   B: That's right. _____ , it's the best film I've ever seen!

6 A: Alex didn't come to the party.

   B: I know, and _____ I'm pleased. He's a really bad boy sometimes!

Discussion box

1 What do you think about running as a sport?
2 When did you last have a pain when doing sport? What happened?

10 Improvisation

Work with a partner. Take two minutes to prepare a short role play. Try to use some of the expressions from Exercise 9a. Do not write the text, just agree on your ideas for a short scene. Then act it out.

Roles: Jess and Joel

Situation: A minute later

Basic idea: Joel has fallen over. Jess is worried.

Use one of these sentences to start the conversation:

Jess: Are you OK?   **Joel:** I can't believe it!

11 Team Spirit ⊙ DVD Episode 5

a Complete the sentences with the words from the box. Use a dictionary if necessary. Then say what you think Episode 5 is about.

b Watch the DVD and see if you were right.

after   celebrate   bet   hold
into   down   ~~compulsory~~

1 This is a _compulsory_ part of the Community Award Scheme.
2 I'm not really _____ sport.
3 I _____ they're brilliant runners.
4 Don't worry. I can look _____ myself.
5 Don't wait for me. I don't want to _____ you up.
6 Do you think she'll let us _____ ?
7 That was fantastic. Now it's time to _____ !

12 Write

a Imagine you got this email from your friend, Spiro, who is studying English in a language school. Why is he unhappy?

Hi ...... (your name),

How are you? I'm not feeling very good at the moment. I'm finding English very difficult. I hate it and I really want to give it up, but my parents say it's important and I have to keep going. I can't speak English very well and I get terrible results in my tests. Have you got any ideas? Help me, please!

Spiro

b Complete the email reply to Spiro. Give him some ideas about learning English. Use some of these phrases.

I think it's a good idea to ...

Try to ...   Remember to ...

Why don't you ...?

... is good/useful/helpful, because ...

... will help you to ...

Hi Spiro

I'm sorry you're feeling bad, but please don't worry about English, and don't give up! I've got some ideas to help you.

....

13 Last but not least: more speaking

Work with a partner.

Student A: Look at the card below.

Student B: Turn to page 126.

Ask questions and answer your partner's to complete the information.

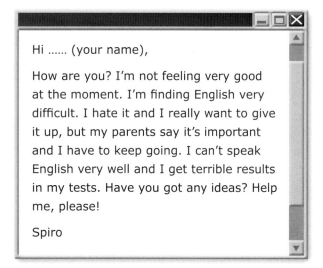

Famous sportsman

Full name: _____

Date of birth: _____

Place of birth: _____

Sport: _____

Began playing when _____ .

In 1995, he started _____ .

In 1999, he _____ .

In 2008, he _____ .

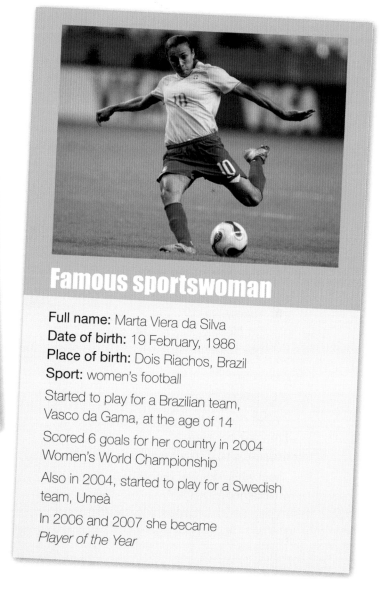

Famous sportswoman

Full name: Marta Viera da Silva
Date of birth: 19 February, 1986
Place of birth: Dois Riachos, Brazil
Sport: women's football

Started to play for a Brazilian team, Vasco da Gama, at the age of 14

Scored 6 goals for her country in 2004 Women's World Championship

Also in 2004, started to play for a Swedish team, Umeå

In 2006 and 2007 she became *Player of the Year*

Check your progress

1 Grammar

a Complete the sentences with *will* or *won't*.

1. My train is running late, so I ___won't___ be home before seven o'clock.
2. Julie isn't feeling well. I don't think she _____ go to school today.
3. He's a really good actor. I'm sure he _____ become famous one day.
4. We can go to the beach tomorrow. I'm sure it _____ rain.
5. What do you think? _____ you go to university?
6. James is in London, so he _____ be at the party tonight.
7. It's quite hot today. I think I _____ go swimming this afternoon.
8. Tom's always so nice. He _____ get angry when he finds out.
9. A: _____ you come to the match tomorrow?

    B: Sorry, but I don't think I _____ have time. I _____ come to the one next week.
10. A: Pat _____ be happy when she sees that you have broken her computer.

    B: I know. I _____ tell her what happened as soon as she comes home.

| 12 |

b Circle the correct words.

1. My parents are *angry* / *angrily* because I didn't do the washing-up.
2. Our team lost yesterday. Everyone played *bad* / *badly*.
3. Last week's test was *easy* / *easily*.
4. My sister sings *good* / *well*.
5. Hurry up, Jill! Why are you walking so *slow* / *slowly*?
6. Last night I heard a *loud* / *loudly* noise outside my room.
7. It was a *slow* / *slowly* journey and we arrived very *late* / *lately*.
8. The players were all too *slow* / *slowly*, that's why we lost the match.
9. His mum works so *hard* / *hardly* – she's *hard* / *hardly* at home.

| 10 |

2 Vocabulary

a Circle the correct words.

1. I'll *probably* / *sure* get a good job.
2. Joanne *doubts* / *hopes* to become a famous singer.
3. *Maybe* / *Don't think* she'll have children.
4. Nick *thinks* / *probably* they'll get married soon.
5. I'm *doubt* / *sure* he'll learn to drive.
6. We'll *doubt* / *probably* watch TV tonight.
7. I *doubt* / *sure* he'll come with us.

| 6 |

b Use the words to complete the sentences.

> lightning foggy shower thunder
> ~~wind~~ hot rain sun

1. There was such a strong ___wind___ that some trees fell down.
2. The castle on that hill burnt down because it was struck by _____ .
3. There was heavy _____ for three days – the streets looked like rivers.
4. It didn't really rain very hard – it was only a _____ .
5. We didn't sit on the beach after 11 am. There was too much _____ and it was too _____ .
6. I've just heard some _____ from far away. I think there'll be a storm soon.
7. I couldn't see anything from my window this morning – it was really _____ outside!

| 7 |

How did you do?

Check your score.

Total score	😊	😐	😞
35	Very good	OK	Not very good
Grammar	19 – 22	16 – 18	less than 16
Vocabulary	11 – 13	9 – 10	less than 9

11 Promises, promises

* *be going to* (intentions and predictions), *must/mustn't*
* Vocabulary: multi-word verbs (2), prepositions

1 Read and listen

a How do you celebrate the New Year in your country?

b Look at the text quickly. Find words or phrases with these meanings:

1 the day before 1 January:
   31 December or ....

2 12 o'clock at night: ....

3 promises people make for the New Year: ....

c Read the text.

d ▶ CD2 T20 Now read the text again and listen. Answer the questions.

1 Where is Times Square?

2 What appears in Times Square just before midnight on 31 December?

3 What do you hear at midnight in Times Square?

4 What happens to many New Year's resolutions?

2 Listen

▶ CD2 T21 Listen to Amy and her dad talking about their New Year's resolutions. Who says what? Write *A* (Amy), or *D* (Dad) next to each sentence.

1 I'm not going to eat unhealthy food any more. ☐

2 I'm going to give up eating chips. ☐

3 Mum and I are going to check out that new gym. ☐

4 I'm going to take up running. ☐

5 We're going to set up a business. ☐

6 I'm sure we can work something out. ☐

In New York for New Year's Eve

It's almost midnight on 31 December, in Times Square, in New York. At 11.59, a sparkling crystal ball appears on the roof of 1 Times Square. The ball takes sixty seconds to drop to the ground. Then the clock strikes twelve and everyone cheers. About a million people in Times Square, millions around the USA and over a billion watching around the world, come together to say 'good bye' to the old year and 'hello' to the new.

In the US, New Year is also a time for thinking about the changes you are going to make in your life. These are called 'New Year's resolutions'. People say, for example, that they are going to give up chocolate or take up exercise. Of course, it's easy to make New Year's resolutions – but it's not so easy to keep them! Unfortunately, many New Year's resolutions have one thing in common: people break them before the New Year is very old!

3 Vocabulary

* Multi-word verbs (2)

▶ CD2 T22 Match the verbs with the definitions. Then listen, check and repeat.

1	take up	a	go to a place to see what it is like
2	give up	b	start doing something
3	look up	c	speak angrily to someone for doing something wrong
4	tell off	d	stop doing something
5	work out	e	find the answer to something
6	check out	f	find out information about something from a book or computer

Vocabulary bank Turn to page 116.

Grammar

✶ be going to: intentions

RULE: We use *be going to* to talk about our intentions in the future (for example, *I'm going to eat more fruit*). We use the present tense of **be** + *going to* + base form of the verb.

a Read the rule and complete the table.

Positive	Negative	Questions	Short answers
I'm (am) going to change	I'm not (am not) going to change	**Am** I going to change?	Yes, I _____ . No, I'm not.
you/we/they 're (are) going to change	you/we/they _____ (are not) going to change	_____ you/we/they going to change?	Yes, you/we/they _____ . No, you/we/they aren't.
he/she/it's (is) going to change	he/she/it _____ (is not) going to change	_____ he/she/it going to change?	Yes, he/she/it is. No, he/she/it _____ .

b Complete the sentences about Amy and her dad. Use the words in the box with the correct form of *be going to*.

> tidy her room every weekend   give up eating chips
> ~~make some changes in their lives~~   start a business
> check out the gym   take up running

1 Amy and her Dad *are going to make some changes in their lives* .

2 Dad _____ .

3 Amy _____ .

4 Mum and Dad _____ .

5 Amy _____ .

6 **Dad:** _____ you and Jodie _____ ?
   Amy: Yes, we _____ .

✶ be going to: predictions

c Read the rule. Then complete the sentences with *be going to* and the verb in brackets.

> **RULE:** We also use *be going to* to make predictions based on what we know or can see (for example, *I think it's going to be an interesting year*).

1 There isn't a cloud in the sky. It *'s going to be* (be) sunny tomorrow.

2 The river is deep here. It _____ (not be) easy to get across.

3 I know they like modern art. They _____ (love) this painting.

4 It's 8.40, Steve! You _____ (be) late!

5 Angela _____ (not get) good results this year. She hardly ever studies at home.

6 _____ we _____ (win) the match?

d Match the sentences with the pictures. Write 1–6 in the boxes.

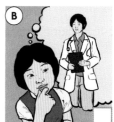

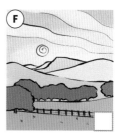

1 He's going to swim.

2 I'm going to cook a great meal tonight!

3 It's going to be a lovely day.

4 They aren't going to eat anything else today!

5 Mum's going to be angry!

6 I'm going to be a doctor when I grow up.

e Which of the sentences in Exercise 4d are intentions? Which are predictions?

5 Speak

a Work with a partner. Together, think of three changes you want to make to your town/city. Write them down.

b Work with someone from another pair. Tell each other what you decided with your first partner.

We're going to put bicycle lanes in …
There's going to be a new shopping centre in …

6 Read and listen

a Kate and Ashley are going to a New Year's Eve party. Look at the first picture. Their parents are talking to them before they go. What do you think their parents are saying?

b ▶ CD2 T23 Listen to Kate and Ashley talking to their parents. Complete the dialogue. Check your ideas.

Kate: Mum? Dad? We're going now, OK?

Mum: OK, you two. Have a good time. But ¹ _____ .

Ashley: Yes, Mum, we know.

Dad: You ² _____ be home at 12.30.

Mum: You can stay at the party for the midnight celebration, but you ³ _____ stay longer than that.

Kate: OK – no problem.

Ashley: It isn't far, so we're ⁴ _____ to leave at 12.15 and ⁵ _____ back. We'll be home at 12.30

Dad: Fine. Have you got your mobile phones?

Mum: Oh, yes, you mustn't ⁶ _____ those.

Kate: We've got mine. Ashley lost his last week, remember?

Mum: OK. Call us if there's any problem, OK?

Ashley: We will – ⁷ _____ .

Dad: OK – off you go. Have a good time

Kate: Thanks. See you later – I ⁸ _____ , at 12.30.

c Look at the second picture. What do you think their parents are going to say?

d ▶ CD2 T24 Why do you think they're home late? Listen and check your ideas.

e ▶ CD2 T24 Put the sentences in the correct order. Listen again and check.

The police came and asked them questions. ☐

They waited with the woman. ☐

They phoned for an ambulance. ☐

The ambulance came. ☐

They left the party. ☐

They saw an accident. ☐

7 Grammar

✳ *must/mustn't*

a Look at the examples. Then complete the rule and the table.

*You **must** be home at 12.30.*

*You **mustn't** stay longer than that.*

RULE: We use _____ when we want to say that it's important to do something.
We use _____ when we want to say that it's important *not* to do something.

Positive	Negative
I/you/we/they/he/she/it _____ go	I/you/we/they/he/she/it _____ (**must not**) go

b Look at the pictures and complete the sentences. Use *must* or *mustn't* and a verb from the box.

stop listen to look touch ~~be~~ miss

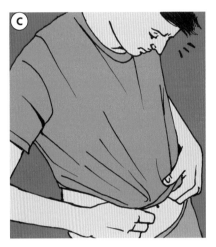

1 I *mustn't be* late for work!

2 I _____ for another job!

3 I _____ eating fried food!

4 You _____ it!

5 We _____ the start of the film!

6 You _____ this CD – it's great!

LOOK!

You **don't have to eat** it = you can eat it if you want to but it isn't obligatory.
You **mustn't eat** it = do not eat it!

8 Pronunciation

 CD2 T25 and T26 Turn to page 111.

Culture in mind

9 Read and listen

a Do you listen to music at these times? Write *Y* (yes) or *N* (no). Then compare with a partner.

when you're doing homework ☐

when you wake up in the morning ☐

when you're walking in the street ☐

when you're feeling sad ☐

when you're feeling happy ☐

when you're eating ☐

b ▶ CD2 T27 Read the text and listen. Answer the questions below.

1 When did reggae become popular?

2 What type of music did reggae develop from?

3 How is reggae different from rock music?

4 What did Jimmy Cliff combine?

5 Who did Bob Marley play with originally?

10 Vocabulary

✴ prepositions

a Complete the sentences with the correct preposition.

1 Music these days is very different __*from*__ 20 years ago.

2 When I hear this song, I always think _____ our last holiday.

3 Rap is not similar _____ reggae.

4 Do you believe _____ the power of music to make you feel happy or sad?

5 A lot of rock music developed _____ rhythm and blues.

6 This is a great song! I'm sure it'll go _____ the charts soon.

b (Circle) the correct word.

1 For me, the (rhythm) / reggae of a piece of music is what's important.

2 Madonna is still making miss / hit records after all this time.

3 Look at the music charts / pops to find out what CD you can buy Emily.

4 What's more important, the music or the blues / lyrics?

5 The style / combination of bass guitar and drums can sound great!

6 We all believe same / equal rights are important, don't we?

Reggae music

Reggae music became a popular musical style more than 50 years ago. When people hear the word 'reggae', they usually think of Jamaica, but in fact, reggae developed in New Orleans, USA, from a type of music called rhythm and blues (R and B). Jamaican musicians changed the beat of R and B and rock music and made a new musical style. It was the beginning of reggae.

Some people say that the reggae beat is similar to the rhythm of the human heartbeat.

It's different from rock music, and is generally easier to sing and dance to. In the 1960s, a lot of young black people wanted to use reggae songs to fight for political freedom and equal rights – for them, the lyrics were very important. But other people wanted reggae to be simply 'good music'. Jimmy Cliff, with his song *Wonderful World, Beautiful People*, was the first person to really bring together reggae music and the 'peace and love' ideas that the hippies of the 1960s believed in.

In the 1960s and the 1970s, there were many reggae bands in the music charts. One of the most famous was the Wailers (Bob Marley, Peter Tosh and Bunny Wailer). Tosh and Wailer left the group but Bob Marley continued to make hit songs like *I Shot The Sheriff* and he became the most famous reggae musician of all time. He died very young, at the age of 36.

11 Listen: a song

 Complete the Jimmy Cliff song with the words in the box. Then listen and check your answers.

> love free helping world secret pretty

Wonderful World, Beautiful People

[Chorus]
Wonderful world, beautiful people
You and your girl, things could be ¹........................
But underneath this there is a ²........................
That nobody can repeat.

Take a look at the ³........................ and the state
that it's in today
I am sure you'll agree we all could make it
a better way
With our ⁴........................ put together everybody
learn to love each other
Instead of fussing and fighting, cheating
but biting
Scandalising and hating.
Baby we could have a ...

[Chorus]

Man and woman, girl and boy, let us try to
give a ⁵........................ hand
This I know and I'm sure that the love we
all could understand
This is our world, can't you see
Everybody wants to live and be ⁶........................
Instead of fussing and fighting, cheating but
biting
Scandalising and hating.
Baby we could have a ...

[Chorus]

12 Speak

Discuss in class.

1 What is the singer worried about?

2 What kind of 'better way' does he want for the world?

3 Do you think that the lyrics of a song are important or just the music?

13 Write

Imagine it's 1 January and you get this email from your Scottish friend, Jessie.

Hi .... (your name)!

Happy New Year! How are you? Did you have a good time last night?

We only had a small party here at home, just my family and a few friends. But it was OK, and I didn't go to bed until 2.00 in the morning.

This email is part of my New Year's resolution – I'm going to write a lot more emails this year! My dad says he's going to give up smoking and go running every morning. He said this last year, but he soon broke his resolution. Have you got any resolutions for this year?

We're on holiday this week, so I'm going to relax and spend some time with my friends. It snowed here yesterday, so we're going to do some snowboarding.

Write soon!

Bye for now,

Jessie

Write an email reply to Jessie. Tell her about:

- your New Year's Eve
- your New Year's resolution(s) and a resolution made by someone in your family
- what you're going to do this week

For your portfolio

What a brave person!

* First conditional, *when* and *if*
* Vocabulary: adjectives of feeling

1 Read and listen

a Look at the pictures. What do you think the text is about?

1 A man who didn't feel well on the platform of a New York subway station.

2 A man who saved another man in the New York subway.

3 The man who designed the platforms of the New York subway.

Read the text quickly and check your answer.

b ▶ CD2 T29 Now read the text again and listen. Answer the questions.

1 Why did Mr Hollopeter fall onto the platform and then the track?

2 How deep was the space where Mr Hollopeter fell?

3 Why did five subway carriages travel over the two men?

4 Who was Mr Autrey worried about when the train stopped?

5 What was the only thing that happened to Mr Autrey?

Subway hero

It was 12.45 p.m. on 2 January, 2007. 50-year-old Wesley Autrey was waiting for the train at a subway station in New York. His two daughters, aged four and six, were with him.

Suddenly, a sick man collapsed on the platform. The man, 20-year-old Cameron Hollopeter, got up, but then fell again – this time, onto the track between the two rails. A train was coming into the station. It was a frightening moment.

But Mr Autrey wasn't frightened. He looked at the man, and he looked at the space that the man was in. It was about half a metre deep. And he thought, 'The train is going to travel over this man. If he tries to get up, the train will kill him. But if he lies on the ground and doesn't move, he'll be OK.' So he knew he had to make a decision.

He jumped. Mr. Autrey lay on top of Mr. Hollopeter, and kept him down on the ground. The train driver saw them. He was terrified, but he couldn't stop in time. Five carriages travelled over the two men before the train stopped.

The people on the platform were shocked. When Mr Autrey heard them screaming, he shouted 'We're OK down here, but I've got two daughters up there. Let them know their father's OK'. People on the platform clapped and cheered – they were amazed at Autrey's courage. Subway workers helped the two men out. An ambulance took Mr. Hollopeter to hospital. He had no serious injuries.

In an interview on a TV show, Mr Autrey said, 'The only thing that happened to me was my blue hat got dirty.'

He added, 'I wasn't brave. I didn't do anything special. I just saw someone who needed help. I did what I thought was right.'

c Do you think Mr Autrey was brave?

d Find words and phrases in the text on page 88 with these meanings.

1 fell down because he was ill (paragraph 2)

2 make a choice about what to do after thinking about several possibilities (paragraph 3)

3 put their hands together to say 'Well done' (paragraph 5)

4 damage to someone's body because of an accident (paragraph 5)

e Tell the class about a time when you were brave.

 Grammar

✱ First conditional

a Match the two halves of the sentences. Check by looking back at the text on page 88.

1 If he tries to get up,   a he'll be OK.

2 If he doesn't move,   b the train will kill him.

b Read the rule and complete the table.

> **RULE:** We use the first conditional to talk about things we think are possible in the future.

If clause	Result clause	
If + present simple	.... (will)	+ base form
	.... (will not)	

c Put the words into the correct order to make sentences.

1 see Jane / if / tell / I / I'll / her

....

2 my parents / I'm / will / if / late / be angry

....

3 I / bring it / I'll / to school tomorrow / if / remember

....

4 you'll / new friend, Jake / come / if / you / meet / my / to the party

....

5 rain tomorrow / if / the / it / doesn't / we'll / to / beach / go

....

d Complete the first conditional sentences with the correct form of the verbs.

1 If Kate ___gives___ (give) me some help, I _'ll finish_ (finish) my homework in an hour.

2 You .... (not meet) anyone if you .... (not go out).

3 I .... (come) to your party if my mum .... (say) I can.

4 If George .... (not want) his ice cream, I .... (eat) it.

5 Susan .... (be) angry if she .... (hear) about this.

6 If we .... (buy) hamburgers, we .... (not have) enough money for the film.

 Speak

Work with a partner.

Student A: Look at the questions below. Student B: Turn to page 126.

Ask your questions and answer your partner's.

Student A

1 What will you do if it rains this weekend?

2 What will you do if the weather's nice?

3 How will you feel if your teacher gives you a lot of homework today?

4 What will you do if you're ill tomorrow?

5 What film will you see if you go to the cinema this week?

6 What programme will you watch if you watch TV this evening?

 Pronunciation

▶ CD2 T30   Turn to page 111.

5 Grammar

✱ *when* and *if*

a What is the difference between sentences 1 and 2? Which speaker is sure he will see John?

1 *I'll give John your message when I see him.*
2 *I'll give John your message if I see him.*

b Complete the sentences with *if* or *when*.

1 I'm seeing Marta tomorrow. I'll ask her about the book ....*when*.... I meet her.

2 A: What are you doing tomorrow?

B: .... there's a good film on, I'll probably go to the cinema.

3 I'm not sure if I want to go to the disco tonight. But .... I decide to go, I'll phone you.

4 It's too hot out in the sun now. Let's play tennis in the evening, ... it's cooler.

6 Vocabulary

✱ Adjectives of feeling

a Look at the examples from the text on page 88. Which adjective describes how the man felt? Which adjective describes the situation?

*It was a **frightening** moment.*
*But Mr Autrey wasn't **frightened**.*

b <u>Underline</u> three more examples of *-ed* adjectives in the text on page 88.

c ▶ CD2 T31 Write the adjectives under the pictures. Then listen, check and repeat.

| tired | bored | ~~excited~~ | interested | annoyed | frightened |

excited

d (Circle) the correct adjective in each sentence.

1 I didn't like the film. I thought it was (boring) / bored.

2 It was a *terrifying / terrified* experience to lose my passport on holiday in a foreign country.

3 My friend, Elena, is really *frightening / frightened* of spiders. She can't stand them!

4 The football match was really *exciting / excited*. In the end Manchester United won 3–2.

5 The lesson wasn't very *interesting / interested*, so some of the students nearly fell asleep.

6 When we saw the film about the bank robbery, we were really *shocked / shocking*.

7 My teacher was very *annoying / annoyed* when I told him I didn't have my homework.

8 I found the marathon really *tiring / tired* – I slept for 12 hours the next day!

Vocabulary bank

Turn to page 116.

7 Listen and speak

a Look at the pictures. Use a word from each box to label the people.

airline   dog   window   steel   ~~X-ray~~   worker   trainer   cleaner   ~~assistant~~   pilot

X-ray assistant

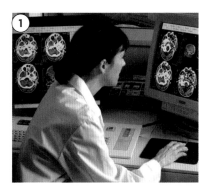

b Which words can go with each picture?

Write the words in the lists.

Nouns:
~~rays~~   temperatures   ~~hospital~~   lift
animals   rope   passengers   fire
airport   teeth

Verbs:
~~make ill~~   land   bite   burn   fall

Picture 1	*rays*	*hospital*	*make ill*
Picture 2			
Picture 3			
Picture 4			
Picture 5			

c How brave do you think the people are? For each picture in Exercise 7a, write a score of 1–5.

(1 = not very brave, 5 = extremely brave).

Picture 1 ....   Picture 2 ....
Picture 3 ....   Picture 4 ....
Picture 5 ....

d ▶ CD2 T32   Listen to Tony and Claudia. Which three pictures are they talking about? Complete the first column of the table.

	Tony	Claudia
Picture __3__	__4__	
Picture		
Picture		

e ▶ CD2 T32   Listen again. Write the scores that Tony and Claudia give to each person.

f Work with a partner. Talk about the scores you gave in Exercise 7c.

A: *What score did you give to the dog trainer? I gave her three. I don't think you have to be brave to work with dogs.*

B: *I don't agree. I gave her five points because …*

Chicken

8 ▶ CD2 T33 **Read and listen**

a Look at the photostory. Debbie is angry because Pete calls her 'chicken'. What do you think he means? Read and listen to find the answer.

1

Miss Bradley: Debbie? The people at Sunny Bank – you know, the home for old people – want someone to give a talk. Could you do it?

Debbie: Me? Stand up and talk? I can't do that.

Miss B: Debbie, it's not a big deal.

2

Jess: Why not, Debbie? I mean, the old people aren't going to laugh or be nasty.

Debbie: No, I know. But ... oh, I don't know. I'm just not brave enough, that's all. I can't do it, and that's that.

Jess: Here she comes. Go on, Pete.

Pete: OK. Well, look – it's yellow Debbie. The school chicken.

Debbie: I beg your pardon?

Pete: I hear you won't give a talk at Sunny Bank. Ooh, all those scary old people! It's a bit pathetic, eh, Debbie?

Debbie: Chicken? Pathetic? No one calls me that!

4

Debbie: Miss Bradley? I've changed my mind. I want to do the talk after all.

Miss B: Good for you, Debbie. How about Friday, around 5 o'clock?

Jess: It worked! Well done, Pete.

Pete: Thanks. But I don't think I can ever talk to Debbie again!

b Mark the statements *T* (true) or *F* (false).

1 The people at Sunny Bank want Debbie to give a presentation. [T]

2 At first, Debbie doesn't want to do a talk. [ ]

3 Jess tells Debbie that she's not brave. [ ]

4 Debbie thinks the old people will laugh at her. [ ]

5 Pete tells Debbie that she's not brave. [ ]

6 Debbie is very angry. [ ]

7 Later, Debbie tells Miss Bradley that she wants to do the talk. [ ]

8 Jess is happy that Pete did what she wanted him to do. [ ]

9 Everyday English

a Find expressions 1–6 in the photostory. Who says them? How do you say them in your language?

1 … not a big deal

2 … and that's that.

3 Go on!

4 I beg your pardon?

5 … after all.

6 Well done.

b Read the dialogues. Use the expressions in Exercise 9a to complete them.

1 **A:** Jenny – please come to the cinema with me!

   B: Listen, Mark – I don't want to go to the cinema with you, [1] *and that's that* . OK?

2 **A:** How did it go at the dentist's today?

   B: It was OK. I was really scared before I went – but it wasn't too bad [2] _____ .

3 **A:** That dress looks horrible!

   B: [3] _____ ?

4 **A:** I heard that you won a skateboarding competition. [4] _____ !

   B: Thanks. But it's [5] _____ – I mean, it was only a small competition.

5 **A:** I think the water's really cold. I don't want to go in!

   B: [6] _____ ! It's OK – it's not *that* cold!

Discussion box

1 Why does Jess say to Pete, 'It worked. Well done!'?

2 How does Pete feel about the situation?

3 In what kind of situation do you feel you 'can't do it'? Does it help if someone calls you 'chicken'? Why (not)?

---

10 Improvisation

Work with a partner. Take two minutes to prepare a short role play. Try to use some of the expressions from Exercise 9a. Do not write the text, just agree on your ideas for a short scene. Then act it out.

Roles: Debbie and Pete

Situation: At school – a few hours later

Basic idea: Debbie sees that Pete doesn't want to talk to her.

Use one of these sentences to start the conversation:

Debbie: Hey, Pete. Can I have a word with you?

Debbie: It's yellow Pete. The school chicken!

11 Team Spirit ⊙ DVD Episode 6

a Match the words and phrases with their definitions.

1 Memory stick

2 IT room

3 video projector

4 entrance hall

5 bulb

6 responsibility

7 permission

8 fault

a a machine that shows films or images on a screen or wall

b mistake

c a small device that stores digital information

d a glass object that produces light

e something that is your job or duty to deal with

f if you are given … to do something, you are allowed to do it

g a computer laboratory

h a big area that you get to when you go into a building

b How does Joel feel? Work with a partner and make a story to explain. Then watch Episode 6 and find out what really happened.

For your portfolio

12 Write

a Read what Geraldine wrote about a book she read. Answer the questions.

1 What was the book?
2 Who was the main character?
3 Where was he/she?
4 Why was he/she in danger?
5 What did he/she do?
6 How did the story end?

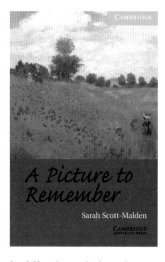

The book I read is *A Picture to Remember* by Sarah Scott-Malden.

It's about a girl called Christina. One day, she saw two men in a car. One of them had a gun. They were bank robbers and she saw their faces. They didn't want her to tell the police, so they planned to kill her.

First, one of the robbers attacked her at the gym, but luckily she only hurt her arm. After this, she was in the street with her friend, Philippe, when one of the robbers drove his car into them. Philippe was hurt and had to go to hospital.

Christina went to visit Philippe. When she left the hospital in her friend's car, the robbers followed her. Christina saw that they had a gun and understood that they wanted to kill her. She was frightened, but she kept calm. The robbers were close behind her, but they were driving too fast and couldn't stop. They crashed their car and it overturned, and the police caught both the robbers.

b Write about a film, book or TV programme where somebody was in a dangerous situation. Use the questions and Geraldine's text to help you.

13 Last but not least: more speaking

a Work alone. Think of a situation you know of when somebody was very brave / not very brave. Take a few minutes to think about the following questions.

- Where was it?
- Who were the people involved?
- What happened? Why was it important for someone to be brave?
- How did you feel in the situation?
- How did the situation end?

b Do a simple drawing of the situation. Here's an example:

c Now work with a partner. Show your partner your drawing. Your partner has ten questions to find out what happened. The questions need to be Yes/No questions.

A: *Did the person in the picture go down the stairs?*
B: *Yes.*
A: *Was it during the night?*
B: *No.*

d If your partner can't guess what happened and has asked all ten questions, tell them about the situation.

Check your progress

1 Grammar

a Complete the sentences. Use the verbs in the box with the correct form of *be going to*.

> visit   help   ~~rain~~   dance   wear
> not ride   not watch

1 Look at those clouds. It*'s going to rain* .

2 I've got a difficult history project to do. My sister _____ me with it.

3 I _____ television tonight. All the programmes are boring!

4 _____ you _____ your black jeans tonight?

5 My parents _____ my grandfather at the weekend.

6 Peter doesn't like horses. He _____ with us this afternoon.

7 There's a party next Friday night, and we _____ all night! | **6**

b Complete each sentence with *must* or *mustn't*.

1 Come on, Julie! We *mustn't* be late!

2 It's a great book. You really _____ read it.

3 Sorry, Jimmy, I'm late. I _____ go now.

4 You _____ tell anyone about this! It's too embarrassing.

5 Diane, turn the music down! You _____ play it so loudly!

6 I can go out with you tonight, but I _____ be home before midnight.

7 OK, you can have a pet snake – but it _____ come into the house! | **6**

c Complete the first conditional sentences with the correct form of the verbs.

1 If you *help* (help) me, I _____ (buy) you an ice cream.

2 If Jack _____ (come) to school late, the teacher _____ (be) really angry.

3 The neighbours _____ (complain) if we _____ (make) a lot of noise.

4 If I _____ (have) time, I _____ (get) the tickets this afternoon. | **7**

2 Vocabulary

a Complete the sentences using the correct multi-word verbs.

1 We're all worried about his health. He should really _____*give up*_____ smoking.

2 If you want to be fit, why don't you _____ some sport?

3 If you don't understand this word, _____ it _____ in a dictionary.

4 It was unfair that the teacher _____ me _____ for talking. It wasn't me who was talking!

5 You don't need to help me with this problem. I think I can _____ it _____ myself.

6 My uncle is a designer. He wants to _____ his own business soon.

7 There's a new youth club in our street. Let's _____ it _____ . | **6**

b Complete the adjectives with the *-ed* or *-ing* ending.

1 I was really tir*ed* last night when I went to bed. Yesterday was a very tir_____ day.

2 We were excit_____ about going to the football, but in the end it was a bor_____ match.

3 I thought the Dracula film was quite frighten_____ , but my girlfriend wasn't frighten_____ at all.

4 We went to a museum last Sunday. My parents thought it was really interest_____ , but I was a bit bor_____ . | **7**

How did you do?

Check your score.

Total score	☺	☺	☹
32	Very good	OK	Not very good
Grammar	15 – 19	12 – 14	less than 12
Vocabulary	11 – 13	8 –10	less than 8

13 Travellers' tales

* *should/shouldn't, What's it like?*
* Vocabulary: personality adjectives, adjectives for expressing opinions

1 Read and listen

a Check that you know the meaning of these words. Match them with the pictures.

1 queue
2 bump into
3 bus stop
4 take off your shoes
5 kiss
6 cover your mouth

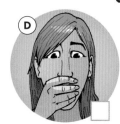

b ▶ CD2 T34 Listen to two people talking about mistakes they made when meeting people from other countries. Make notes to answer the questions:

1 Who are the other people involved?
2 What mistake(s) did the speaker or other people make in each situation?

c Have you ever made a similar mistake? Where were you? Who were you with? What happened?

d Read the questions in the quiz. What do you think? Write *T* (true) or *F* (false).

e ▶ CD2 T35 Listen and check your answers.

Quiz: what do you know about UK culture?

1 If you bump into someone, even by accident, you should say 'Sorry'. ☐

2 You should go to the front of the queue at a bus stop or ticket office. ☐

3 You should always take your shoes off when you go into someone's house. ☐

4 You should always kiss someone when you meet them for the first time. ☐

5 If someone invites you for dinner, you shouldn't arrive early. ☐

6 You shouldn't talk if you have food in your mouth. ☐

2 Grammar

✳ *should/shouldn't*

a Look at the examples and read the rule. <u>Underline</u> examples of *should* and *shouldn't* in the quiz.

*You **should** go to the front of the queue at a bus stop or ticket office.*
*You **shouldn't** talk if you have food in your mouth.*

> **RULE:** We use *should* or *shouldn't* to say 'It's a good idea' or 'It isn't a good idea'.

b Complete the table.

Positive	Negative	Questions	Short answers
I/you/we/they/he/she/it **should** go	I/you/we/they/he/she/it _____ (**should not**) go	**Should**/I/you/we/they/ he/ she/it go?	Yes, I/you/we/they/he/she/it _____ . No, /you/we/they/he/she/it _____ (**should not**).

c Complete the dialogues. Use *should* or *shouldn't* and a verb from the box.

go   watch   wear

1   **Steve:** I don't know which jacket to wear.
    Paul: The white one's great. I think you *should wear* that one.

2   **Jane:** There's a programme about Japan on TV tonight.
    Tim: Really? Then I _____ it. I'm doing a project on Japan.

3   **Alex:** My eyes really hurt. _____ I _____ to the doctor?
    Father: No, but you _____ television so much, Alex.

4   **Amy:** I'm tired.
    Lucy: Me too. It's nearly 11.30. I think we _____ to bed.

5   **Anna:** What do you think? _____ I _____ jeans to the party this evening?
    Carol: No, everybody's wearing party clothes. You _____ your long dress.

6   **Peter:** Mum, I feel awful this morning.
    Mother: Yes, you look ill. Perhaps you _____ to school today.

7   You should always cover your mouth with your hand when you laugh. ▢

8   When you are staying with a family and someone offers you food, you should always say 'No thank you' three times before accepting, even if you are very hungry. ▢

HA-HA-HA!

3 Speak

Work with a partner.
Student A: Read the role card below.
Student B: Turn to page 126 and read the role card.
Take it in turns to listen to your partner's problem and give advice with *should* or *shouldn't*.

> **Student A**
>
> You play the guitar in a band. You practise for about two hours every evening, so you don't have time to do all your schoolwork. Your parents are annoyed because your test results are bad. They want you to leave the band and do your schoolwork. You are very unhappy because you love playing in the band, but you want to get good school results too. Should you stay in the band? Should you leave? Ask Student B.

4 Vocabulary

✱ Personality adjectives

a ▶ CD2 T36 Listen and repeat the adjectives. Check that you understand their meaning.

kind   hard-working   polite   honest   organised   ~~cheerful~~   relaxed   friendly

b Complete the sentences with the adjectives in Exercise 4a.

1 A _cheerful_ person is usually happy and smiles a lot.

2 An .... person tells you what he/she really thinks.

3 A .... person doesn't worry about things.

4 A .... person works a lot.

5 An .... person is tidy and keeps things in order.

6 A .... person helps people and thinks about their feelings.

7 A .... person is easy to talk to and makes friends easily.

8 A .... person always says *please* and *thank you*.

c ▶ CD2 T37 Write the adjectives under the pictures. Then listen, check and repeat.

unfriendly   dishonest   unkind   lazy   miserable   nervous   rude   disorganised

 (A)    (B)    (C)    (D)

 (E)    (F)    (G)    (H)

d Complete the table of opposites.

Adjectives	Opposites
1 kind	_unkind_
2 cheerful	....
3 polite	....
4 honest	....
5 organised	....
6 relaxed	....
7 hard-working	....
8 friendly	....

e Complete the sentences with adjectives. Use your own ideas.

1 I think I'm a/an .... person.

2 My best friend is .... and ....

3 Our neighbours are very ....

4 I don't like people who are ....

Vocabulary bank Turn to page 117.

Turn to page 117.

5 Pronunciation

▶ CD2 T38 and T39 Turn to page 111.

Turn to page 111.

6 Grammar

✱ *What's it like?*

a Match the questions with the answers.

1 What was the weather like on your holiday? [d]
2 What's your new teacher like? [ ]
3 What are the people like in New York? [ ]
4 What were the films like last night? [ ]
5 What's this CD like? [ ]

a They're very friendly and helpful.
b It's brilliant! You should listen to it.
c Well, I thought they were a bit boring.
d Awful! It rained all the time.
e She's nice and she's really funny!

b When we ask for an opinion about something or someone, we can ask: *What* + *be* + subject + *like*? Look at the questions in Exercise 6a and complete the table.

What	is	he / .... / it	.................?
	....		
	....	they	
	were		

c Write the questions. Use the words in brackets.

1 A: I went to Greece last year.
   B: Really? What _was it like_ ? (it)
2 A: I've got the new Mariah Carey CD.
   B: Oh? What _____ ? (it)
3 A: There's a new girl in our class.
   B: A new girl? What _____ ? (she)
4 A: We visited Spain a few weeks ago.
   B: Oh, that's nice! What _____ ? (the weather)
5 A: I've got some new trainers.
   B: Really? What _____ ? (they)
6 A: I read three books last week.
   B: Wow! What _____ ? (they)

7 Vocabulary

✱ Adjectives for expressing opinions

a ▶ CD2 T40 Here are some adjectives we can use to give an opinion. Write them in the columns. Then listen, check and repeat.

~~boring~~   ~~brilliant~~   interesting   attractive
fantastic   awful   cool   dull   ugly   dreadful

+ (positive)	– (negative)
brilliant	boring

b Which adjectives from Exercise 7a can you use to describe:

1 a film?   3 a city/town?   5 the weather?
2 a person?   4 a party?

8 Speak

a Work with a partner. Ask and answer questions about the things in the box.

your brother/sister/parents/boyfriend/girlfriend
your town or city   your home   your last holiday
your favourite singer   your last weekend

A: *What's your brother like?*
B: *He's OK sometimes. He's ....*

b Work with a different partner.

Student A has 1 minute to think of as many different questions as possible using '*What's ... like?*' Student A asks Student B the questions. Student B listens but doesn't answer.

Then Student B has one minute to remember the questions and answer them. He/she thinks of one 'wrong' answer. When Student B finishes, Student A guesses the wrong answer.

Culture in mind

9 Read and listen

a Look through the text quickly and find answers to the following questions.

1 Who is the man in the picture?
2 What's his job?
3 Where is he from?

b ▶ CD2 T41 Read and listen to the text and check your answers.

c Find words in the text that mean:

1 the line on a map that separates two countries (paragraph 2)
2 a place where people live, smaller than a town (paragraph 2)
3 with no shoes on (paragraph 3)
4 an international football competition (paragraph 4)
5 in another country (paragraph 5)
6 the situation of being very poor (paragraph 5)

Heroic Ulises on a journey of hope

Tourists go to Ecuador to go whale or bird watching, to visit the Amazon Rainforest, or to go to the Galapagos Islands, one of the world's most famous nature paradises.

But not many tourists go to the village of Piquiucho in the Chota Valley. It is near the Colombian border, about three hours drive north of the capital, Quito. Life for people in this village is hard, and many of them haven't got houses, only simple huts. But there's something very special about Piquiucho: half of the footballers who played for Ecuador in the World Cup in 2002 and 2006 (a total of 11 players) came from this poor village.

Piquiucho was the starting point for one man's journey of hope. Ulises de la Cruz started to play football barefoot as a child. His dream was to become a professional football player. And one day his dream came true. He played for his national team, and later in the English Premier League.

He earned a lot of money, but he didn't spend his money on fast cars and big houses. When Ecuador reached the World Cup finals in 2002, Ulises used the money he earned to buy a fresh water supply for Piquiucho. He used the money he made from playing for Ecuador in the 2006 World Cup to help the people of his village too, 'The 2006 World Cup in Germany was fantastic because it meant I could give money for a new sports and community centre,' he said.

10 Speak

Discuss in groups.

1 Which facts about Ecuador are new to you? Which ones did you already know?

2 What is your reaction to the story about Ulises de la Cruz?

3 Do you think what he does is 'heroic'? Why/why not?

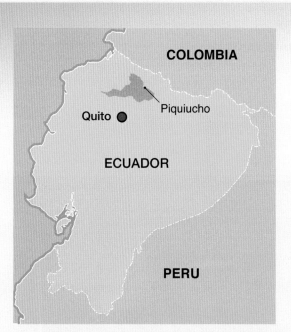

COLOMBIA

Piquiucho

Quito ●

ECUADOR

PERU

He pays for breakfast and lunch for 100 school children every day. Since he started to play abroad, he has sent hundreds of thousands of pounds back to his village. He has set up a medical centre there, and he pays for a doctor, a dentist and a nurse. 'I want to help the children of Piquiucho. I want to show them that they have a better future. I want to show them that by studying, they can help themselves to escape poverty. Football isn't the only way out.'

11 Write

a Jill's e-pal Mathilde, is visiting Britain in March. Read Jill's email and match the topics with the paragraphs.

a Things that Mathilde should/shouldn't do in Britain. ☐

b Things that Mathilde should take to Britain. ☐

c British people. ☐

Hi Mathilde

I'm really happy you're coming to visit us here in Britain. I'm writing to tell you some things about my country.

1 First, I'm sure you're going to like the people here. They're usually friendly and helpful.

2 Remember to bring an umbrella and a raincoat. It often rains a lot in March and April. You should bring some warm clothes, too.

3 Don't forget, you should always say 'please' and 'thank you' when you ask for something. And you shouldn't go to the front of a queue – people hate that here!

I can't wait to see you!

Love,

Jill

---

b Work with a partner. Make a list of useful tips for British tourists who are coming to visit your country.

c Imagine that your English-speaking e-pal is visiting your country soon. Write a similar email to him/her.

For your portfolio

14 Crazy records

* Present perfect + *ever/never*
* Vocabulary: verb and noun pairs, expressions about *sleep*

1 Read and listen

a Read the texts quickly. Match them with the pictures.

b ▶ CD2 T42 Now read the texts again and listen. One of the texts has facts that are incorrect. Which one, do you think? Listen and check.

c What do you think about these records? Tell others in your class.

You've never seen anything like this!

People do some unusual things, and some of them have appeared in the record books. Here are a few examples. Have you ever seen anything as strange as this?

1 Saimir Strati from Albania built the largest picture ever made from toothpicks. The artist used 1.5 million toothpicks and worked 40 days to do it.

2 On 25 September, 2005, 637 people in gorilla suits ran a 'fun run' in London, to raise money for *The Dian Fossey Gorilla Fund*. It was the largest group of people dressed as gorillas that has ever come together.

3 The people at Miniature Wunderland in Hamburg, Germany, have constructed the longest model train in the world. It has three locomotives and 887 cars and measures 110 metres! How long would a real train of this size be? The answer: almost 10 kilometres!

4 Have you ever seen a motor cycle that's bigger than you? Well, here's one! Gregory Dunham (USA) has built the world's biggest motorcycle. It is 2.4 m tall, about 4 m long and weighs about 1 ton. Has Gregory ever ridden it? Yes, he has, and he says it's great fun!

A

B

C

D

2 Grammar

★ Present perfect + *ever/never*

a Look at the examples. Complete the rule and the table.

*Some people **have appeared** in the record books.*
***Have** you ever **seen** anything as strange as this?*
*He's **never** cut it.*

> **RULE:** We use the present perfect to talk about actions that happened some time up to now.
>
> We form the present perfect with the present tense of .... + past participle.

Positive	Negative	Questions	Short answers
I/you/we/they **'ve** (__have__) work**ed**	I/you/we/they (...............) **(have not)** work**ed**	.... I/you/we/they work**ed**?	Yes, I/you/we/they **have**. No, I/you/we/they **haven't**.
he/she/it **'s** (...............) work**ed**	he/she/it **hasn't** (...............) work**ed**	...............he/she/it work**ed**?	Yes, he/she/it **has**. No, he/she/it **hasn't**.

b Fill in the verb forms. Use the Irregular verbs list on page 127 to help you.

Base form	Past participle
1 be	_been_
2 do	....
3 go	....
4 see	....
5 write	....
6 bite	....
7 speak	....
8 eat	....
9 drive	....
10 fly	....
11 swim	....
12 win	....

LOOK!

He **has gone** to New York.
= He is not here now –
he is in New York.

He **has been** to New York.
= At some time in the past,
he went to New York
and came back.

c Complete the sentences. Use the present perfect form of the verbs.

1 We _'ve never lived_ (never / live) in a foreign country.
2 I .... (never / see) a tarantula.
3 .... you .... (ever / drive) a car?
4 Sorry, Jane isn't here – she .... (go) to the cinema.
5 Jack .... (be) to Japan, but he .... (never / eat) sushi.

3 Pronunciation

▶ CD2 T43 Turn to page 111.

4 Speak

a Work with a partner. Ask and answer the questions.

1 ever / see / a tiger?
2 ever / eat / Chinese food?
3 ever / be / on TV?
4 ever / speak / to a British person?
5 ever / win / any money?
6 ever / be / to London?

A: *Have you ever seen a tiger?*
B: *No, never. Have you ever eaten Chinese food?*
A: *Yes, I have.*

b Work with a partner or in a small group. Ask and answer questions about things you have done in your life. Use some of the verbs in the box.

travel   stay   play   win   eat   fly   drive   meet

5 Vocabulary

✱ Verb and noun pairs

a Look at this example of a verb and noun pair from the text in Exercise 1 on page 102.

*They ran a 'fun run' to **raise money** for The Dian Fossey Gorilla Fund.*

Match the verbs with the nouns.

Verbs	Nouns
1 raise	a a risk
2 win	b a prize
3 break	c a joke
4 build	d a record
5 tell	e money
6 take	f a house

b Complete the sentences. Use verbs from Exercise 5a in the correct form.

1 In the 1968 Olympics long jump, Bob Beamon ____won____ the gold medal, and he _____ the world record.

2 At the moment, Sandro's parents _____ _____ a new house.

3 The charity, Oxfam, _____ lots of money every year for poor people.

4 Esra _____ a risk when she rode her bike without a helmet.

5 I like Steve because he _____ really good jokes.

c Underline the verb + noun combination in each sentence.

1 I'm tired now – I think I'll <u>do</u> my <u>homework</u> tomorrow morning.

2 Sorry, he can't talk to you now, he's having a shower.

3 My grandfather tells really good stories about when he was young.

4 My mum isn't feeling well, so I'm going to make dinner tonight.

5 Tonight I'm going to spend a bit of time with my friends.

6 My brother is taking a very important exam today.

Vocabulary bank Turn to page 117.

6 Read

a Look at the pictures. Which one shows:

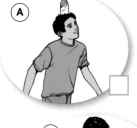

1 juggling
2 doing the hula-hoop
3 balancing a bottle on your head
4 skipping
5 balancing an egg on a spoon

b Read the text quickly. Which thing in Exercise 6a is not mentioned in the text?

He holds the record – for records!

Ashrita Furman has always been interested in Guinness World Records. As a teenager, he spent a lot of time reading the book and today, he is the holder of the most amazing record of all: he has appeared in *The Guinness Book of World Records* 203 times.

Most of his records involve physical activity. For example, he has walked 103 kilometres while balancing a milk bottle on his head! It took him 23 hours and 35 minutes. He has also pushed a car just over 27 kilometres in 24 hours.

A few years ago, Furman set three new records in less than an hour on the same day. First, he ran a mile in 12 minutes and 15 seconds – while doing the hula-hoop. A few minutes later, he ran a mile balancing a raw egg on a spoon in seven minutes and 47 seconds. And then he set a new record for juggling while standing on a pogo stick for 24 minutes and 48 seconds. These were Furman's 115th, 116th, and 117th Guinness World Records. And he hasn't finished. Furman's life is all about breaking records, and by the time you read this, he's probably already broken a few more!

c Read the text again. Answer the questions.

1 How many records has Furman broken?
2 How far has he walked with a bottle on his head?
3 How long did it take him to break three records on the same day?

7 Listen

a Which of these things do you think are the hardest to do? Discuss with a partner.

- not eat anything for three days
- not open your eyes for three days
- not sleep for three days
- not sit down for three days

b What do you think is the world record for not sleeping?

a 8 days   b 11 days
c 13 days   d 16 days

c ▶ CD2 T44 Listen to a conversation between Matthew and Grace. Check your answer to Exercise 7b.

d ▶ CD2 T44 Listen again and answer the questions.

1 What article have Matthew and Grace read?
2 What does Grace think about the person in the article?
3 What does Grace say Matthew does after 30 minutes at school?
4 What does Matthew say he does in lessons?
5 When did the American man set the world record for not sleeping?
6 How long did the American man sleep after he broke the record?

8 Vocabulary

✱ expressions about *sleep*

a ▶ CD2 T45 Look at the expressions about sleep. Match the opposites. Then listen, check and repeat.

1 to go to bed   a to wake up
2 to go to sleep   b to be awake
3 to be asleep   c to get up

b What's the difference between *dreaming* and *daydreaming*?

c Complete the sentences with the expressions in the box. Use the correct form of the verbs. You can check with the list of irregular verbs on page 127.

> wake up   go to sleep   ~~go to bed~~   be asleep
> get up   be awake   dream   daydream

1 My mother was very tired last night. She _went to bed_ at nine o'clock.
2 Sometimes I go to bed at ten. Then I read a book for an hour and I _____ at about eleven.
3 Last night Lucy _____ about winning the lottery.
4 Please talk quietly. The baby _____ .
5 I didn't sleep at all last night. I _____ all night.
6 This morning I _____ at six o'clock, but I'm lazy, so I stayed in bed and I _____ at eight.
7 Nick doesn't listen to the teacher. He _____ about being a famous singer.

9 Speak

a Complete each of these questions. Write one word in each space.

1 What time do you usually _go_ to bed during the week?
2 Do you sometimes read in bed before you go to _____ ?
3 What time do you usually get _____ during the week?
4 When you _____ up, do you usually get up immediately?
5 When you _____ , do you often remember it when you wake up?
6 Do you look out of the window and _____ ?

b Work with a partner. Ask and answer the questions.

What's the next thing?

10 Read and listen

a ▶ CD2 T46   Look at the title. What do you think Jess, Debbie, Joel and Pete are talking about? Read and listen to find the answer.

1

Debbie: Know what I'm thinking?

Joel: What's that, Debbie?

Debbie: We should go to the café. We haven't been there for a while.

Jess: Pete and I went there a few weeks ago.

2

Pete: That's right. We did. Jess ate a huge ice cream!

Jess: Careful Pete!

Pete: Just joking, Jess! Tell you what, I'll pay for the drinks today!

Joel: That's what I like to hear!

3

Jess: This is such good fun. We should come here more often.

Joel: That's right.

Jess: By the way – what's the next thing in the English project?

Pete: We have to talk about our hobbies.

Joel: Oh yes. What are you going to talk about, Pete?

Pete: Wait and see!

4

Joel: I'm going to talk about pet snakes – and I'm taking my own pet snake along.

Jess: Snakes? No, please, I hate them!

Pete: I think he's joking, Jess.

Debbie: Oh Joel – you're such a clown!

b Match. Then put the sentences in the correct order. Write 1–6 in the boxes.

a ☐ Jess changes the subject and asks   1 a pet snake, but he's only joking.

b ☐ Debbie thinks   2 what they have to do in the next English project.

c ☐ Joel says he's got   3 talk about their hobbies.

d ☐ Pete says they have to   4 to buy drinks for everyone.

e ☐ Pete doesn't tell them   5 they should go to the café again.

f ☐ Pete offers   6 what he's going to talk about.

11 Everyday English

a Find expressions 1–6 in the photostory. Who says them? How do you say them in your language?

1   ... for a while.
2   Careful!
3   Tell you what, ...
4   (This is) such good fun.
5   By the way, ...
6   Wait and see!

b Read the dialogues. Use the expressions in Exercise 11a to complete them.

1   A: What are you going to give me for my birthday?
    B: ¹ _Wait and see!_

2   A: I'm hungry.
    B: Me too. ² .... , let's go to the café and get a sandwich.

3   A: I really like Sarah.
    B: So do I. She's
        ³ .... ! And she tells great jokes, too.

4   A: Hi Joe! I haven't seen you for ages.
    B: I know. I was ill
        ⁴ .... , but I'm better now.

5   A: Wow! This song's awful!
    B: ⁵ .... ! This is my favourite band's new record!

6   A: That was a great party last night.
    B: It was – really great!
        ⁶ .... , I'm having a party next week. Do you want to come?

Discussion box

1   In what situations do you enjoy laughing and making jokes with your friends?

2   How do you feel if someone plays the clown <u>all</u> the time?

---

12 Improvisation

Work with a partner. Take two minutes to prepare a short role play. Try to use some of the expressions from Exercise 11a. Do not write the text, just agree on your ideas for a short scene. Then act it out.

Roles: Debbie and Joel

Situation: They are on the phone a few hours later

Basic idea: Debbie wants to play a joke on Joel. She has an idea and phones him.

Use one of these sentences to start the conversation:

Debbie: Hi Joel. Guess what?

Debbie: Oh, Joel, I was wondering if you could help me get my talk ready?

13 Team Spirit ⦿ DVD Episode 7

a What does picture 1 show?

a   ballet dancing
b   classical dancing
c   line dancing
d   disco dancing

b Which of these do you think is Pete's hobby? Look at picture 2. What do Jess and Debbie think of it?

c Watch Episode 7 and find out.

14 Write

a Imagine you are staying with an American family in Los Angeles. You have received this email from an English-speaking friend. What topics does she ask about?

b Write an email or letter in reply to Louise. Start like this:

Dear Louise,

Thanks for your email and the photo. It was great to hear from you.

I'm having a fantastic time here in Los Angeles.

Dear .... (your name),

How are you? Are you enjoying yourself in Los Angeles? I hope your journey there was OK, and you weren't too tired when you arrived.

Please tell me all about the family you're staying with. What are they like? What have you done and seen in Los Angeles? Have you met any interesting people? Have you visited Hollywood and have you seen any film stars?

I'm having a good time. I've started horse-riding lessons, so I'm sending a photo of me on Fury, one of the horses at our riding school. I've also finished all my exams (great!) and my sister has passed her driving test, so now she can drive me everywhere!

Write soon, OK?

Love,

Louise

15 Last but not least: more speaking

a Complete each of these sentences with something that is true for you. Use the pictures to help you with ideas.

b Work in pairs or groups. Tell other students about your sentences. Ask them about theirs.

A: *I've never been to New York, but I really want to go one day!*

B: *Why do you want to go to New York?*

A: *I'm sure it's a really cool city.*

B: *OK. My turn. I've never touched a snake, and I don't think I ever will.*

A: *Why?*

B: *I think they're fantastic animals, but there aren't any snakes in this country!*

1 I've never _____ , but I really want to!

2 I've never _____ , and I really don't want to!

3 I've never _____ , but I'm sure that I will in the future.

4 I've never _____ , and I don't think that I ever will.

Check your progress

1 Grammar

a Complete the sentences with *should* or *shouldn't*.

1 You *shouldn't* eat a lot of fried food.

2 I _____ do more exercise. I'd like to be fitter.

3 When you wait for a bus in Britain, you _____ stand in the queue.

4 They _____ get some exercise. They _____ spend so much time in front of the computer.

5 You look great! You _____ worry about losing weight!

6 Maria is feeling ill. _____ we take her to the doctor?

6

b Write sentences in the present perfect.

1 I / never / see / a tarantula.

I've never seen a tarantula.

2 My brother / never / study / a foreign language.

_____ .

3 My parents / never / fly / in a plane.

_____ .

4 I / never / get / 100% in a test.

_____ .

5 Richard / never / eat / frogs' legs.

_____ .

6 your teacher / ever / shout / at you?

_____ ?

7 you / ever / speak / to a British person?

_____ ?

8 your parents / ever / win / a competition?

_____ ?

7

2 Vocabulary

a Write the opposites of the adjectives.

1 honest   *dishonest*

2 kind   _____

3 organised   _____

4 cheerful   _____

5 friendly   _____

6 polite   _____

7 hard-working _____

8 relaxed   _____

7

b Complete the sentences with the correct verb from the box. Change the form when necessary.

> raise   build   spend
> ~~break~~   do   tell   have

1 He is a good runner, but he will never *break* a record.

2 At school we are trying to _____ money for a family whose house burnt down.

3 Stop _____ jokes now. We really have other things to do.

4 It only took them three months to _____ the house.

5 I'm so hot. I'd like to _____ a shower.

6 He _____ hours watching TV every night. How silly!

7 Sorry, I've got no time. I need to _____ my homework now.

6

How did you do?

Check your score.

Total score	🙂 Very good	😐 OK	🙁 Not very good
26			
Grammar	11 – 13	8 – 10	less than 8
Vocabulary	11 – 13	8 – 10	less than 8

Unit 1 /n/ (ma<u>n</u>) and /ŋ/ (so<u>ng</u>)

a ▶ CD1 T9 Listen and repeat the words.

/n/ man fun town Japan Britain Italian
/ŋ/ thing song sing morning writing

b ▶ CD1 T10 Listen and repeat the sentences.

1 Jenny likes dancing and painting.
2 Dan enjoys running in the morning.
3 We sing songs for fun.

Unit 2 /ɜː/ (w<u>or</u>ld)

a ▶ CD1 T13 Listen and repeat the words.

her world work learn birthday university

b ▶ CD1 T14 Listen and repeat the sentences.

1 All over the world.
2 He always works hard.
3 Learn these words!
4 They weren't at university.

Unit 3 *was* and *were*

a ▶ CD1 T20 Listen to the sentences. What vowel sound do you hear? Listen again and repeat.

1 Erin was an American woman.
2 There were a lot of papers.
3 Was the water clean?
4 Were the people sick?

b ▶ CD1 T21 Listen and tick (✓) the vowel sound you hear. Then listen again and repeat.

	/ɒ/	/ɜː/	/ə/
1 I was unhappy.	☐	☐	☐
2 We were late yesterday.	☐	☐	☐
3 Was it noisy?	☐	☐	☐
4 Yes, it was.	☐	☐	☐

-ed endings

c ▶ CD1 T22 Listen to the sentences. Write the words in bold in the lists.

1 We **walked** a long way.
2 We **visited** an interesting museum.
3 I **used** a red pen to do the test.
4 We **wanted** another hamburger.
5 I **watched** a great programme last night.
6 My painting was awful, so I **started** again.

/d/ or /t/	/ɪd/
walked	*visited*

Unit 4 Word stress

a ▶ CD1 T28 Look at the list. How many syllables has each word got? Listen and check.

1 surfing   3 sport   5 skateboarding
2 basketball   4 cycling   6 champion

b ▶ CD1 T28 Write the words in the lists. Then listen again and check.

●   ●●   ●●●

_____   _____   _____

            _____   _____

                        _____

Unit 5 *have to / don't have to*

Usually, *have* has a /v/ sound, but in *have to / don't have to*, it has a /f/ sound. Also *to* has the weak sound /ə/.

▶ CD1 T33 Listen and repeat the sentences.

1 I have to go.
2 You don't have to shout.
3 He doesn't have to come.
4 We have to learn English.

Unit 6 The schwa /ə/ (wat<u>er</u>)

a ▶ CD1 T40 The most common vowel sound in English is /ə/. Listen and repeat.

water sugar tomato banana
exercise vegetable

b ▶ CD1 T41 Listen and underline the syllables with the /ə/ sound. Then listen again and repeat.

a carrot an orange some bread
some apples some onions a lot of fruit
a lot of calories a lot of vegetables

Unit 7 *than*

a ▶ CD1 T47 Listen to the sentences and <u>underline</u> the stressed syllables.

1 Pronunciation is more difficult than grammar.
2 Spanish is easier than German.
3 My speaking is better than my writing.
4 Is French more interesting than English?

b How do you pronounce *than*? Listen again and repeat.

Unit 8 /θ/ (th<u>i</u>nk) and /ð/ (th<u>a</u>t)

a ▶ CD2 T5 Listen and repeat the words.

1 think   three   month   something   toothache
2 that   those   with   brother   sunbathing

b ▶ CD2 T6 Listen and repeat the phrases. <u>Underline</u> *th* when the sound is /θ/. (Circle) *th* when the sound is /ð/.

1 Give me those things.
2 There's nothing in my mouth.
3 I think it's Thursday.

Unit 9 '*ll*

▶ CD2 T10 Listen and tick (✓) the sentence you hear.

1 a   I ask the teacher.
   b   I'll ask the teacher.
2 a   They go to school early.
   b   They'll go to school early.
3 a   We have a lot of work to do.
   b   We'll have a lot of work to do.
4 a   I go to London by train.
   b   I'll go to London by train.

Unit 10 /əʊ/ (g<u>o</u>)

a ▶ CD2 T16 Listen and repeat the words.

show   no   homework   clothes
boat   snow

b ▶ CD2 T17 Listen to the sentences. <u>Underline</u> the words or syllables that have the /aʊ/ sound. Then listen again, check and repeat.

1 She was the only person who survived.
2 She walked slowly along the river.
3 The plane exploded.
4 When she woke up, she was alone.

Unit 11 *must* and *mustn't*

a ▶ CD2 T25 *Must* is usually stressed, and sometimes the stress is very strong. Listen and repeat. Which sentences put a strong stress on *must*? Why?

1 I must go to the post office later.
2 You must work harder.
3 You must come to my party!

b ▶ CD2 T26 Listen to these sentences. Notice the pronunciation of *mustn't*: /ˈmʌsənt/. Listen again and repeat.

1 You mustn't eat that!
2 We mustn't forget.
3 You mustn't drive too fast.

c Say the sentences from Exercise b. Listen and check.

Unit 12 Stress in conditional sentences

a ▶ CD2 T30 Listen to the sentences. Which words are stressed? Why? <u>Underline</u> the stressed words or syllables.

1 If it rains, I won't go to the beach.
2 We won't pass the test if we don't work hard.
3 I'll give him the card if I see him.
4 If you decide to come, I'll meet you at the cinema.
5 She won't arrive on time if she misses the train.

b Listen again and repeat.

Unit 13 Silent consonants

a ▶ CD2 T38 Listen and repeat the words. In each word below, there is a 'silent' consonant which we don't pronounce. <u>Underline</u> the silent consonants.

1 honest   2 should   3 school
4 write   5 climb   6 know   7 two

b ▶ CD2 T39 Which consonants are silent in these words? Listen, check and repeat.

1 shouldn't   2 wrong   3 foreign
4 listen   5 island   6 fascinating

Unit 14 *have* and *has* in the present perfect

▶ CD2 T43 How are *have* and *has* pronounced? Listen again and repeat.

A: *Have you ever driven a car?*
B: *Yes, I have.*

A: *Has she ever studied a foreign language?*
B: *Yes, she has.*

Unit 1 hobbies and interests

1 keeping a diary

6 collecting (stickers/stamps/coins)

2 bird-watching

7 drawing pictures

3 hanging out with friends

8 making models

4 going for walks

9 fishing

5 looking after a (cat/dog/rabbit)

10 doing puzzles

Unit 2 rooms and housework

1 a pillow	4 a (cleaning) cloth	7 (book) shelves	10 drawers	13 (clothes) hangers
2 a duvet	5 a mop	8 a magazine rack	11 a cupboard	14 a (waste) bin
3 a vacuum cleaner	6 a bucket	9 a CD rack	12 a wardrobe	15 a poster

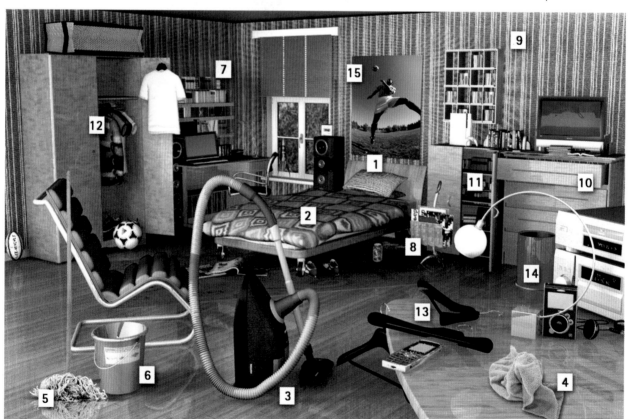

Unit 3 multi-word verbs (1) (with *up, down, on, off*)

 1   to get up

 2   to stand up

 3   to sit down

 4   to lie down

 5   to get on

 6   to get off

 7   to switch on

 8   to switch off

Unit 4 sports equipment and places

 1   a helmet

 2   (cricket/boxing/ cycling/goalie) gloves

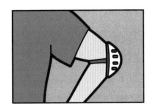 3   (knee/elbow/ shin) pads

 4   a (squash/tennis/ badminton) racket

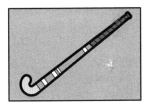 5   a (hockey/lacrosse/ polo) stick

 6   (football/rugby) boot

 7   (football/tennis/ rugby) shorts

 8   (football/tennis/ rugby) shirt

 9   a (surf/skate) board

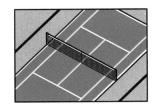 10   a (tennis/squash/ volleyball) court

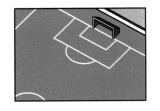 11   a (football/rugby/ baseball) pitch

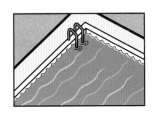 12   (swimming/diving) pool

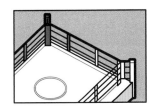 13   a (boxing) ring

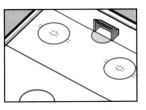 14   a (skating/ice-hockey) rink

 15   a gym

Unit 5 work

1 (to work) at home

2 (to work) in an office

3 (to work) in a shop

4 (to work) in a factory

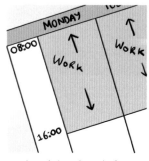

5 (to do) a day shift

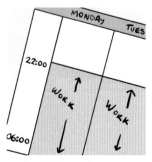

6 (to do) a night shift

7 (to earn) wages

8 (to earn) a salary

Unit 6 food / things we use to eat and drink

1 a knife

2 a fork

3 a spoon

4 a plate

5 a glass

6 a bowl

7 a napkin

8 a cup

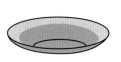

9 a saucer

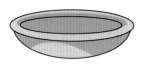

10 a dish

11 a straw

12 chopsticks

13 a mug

14 a menu

Unit 8 holiday activities

1. taking photographs
2. going to a market
3. looking at a view
4. visiting monuments
5. trying local food
6. meeting local people
7. buying souvenirs
8. trying out the language
9. going on an excursion
10. learning local customs
11. visiting a theme park
12. learning about history and culture

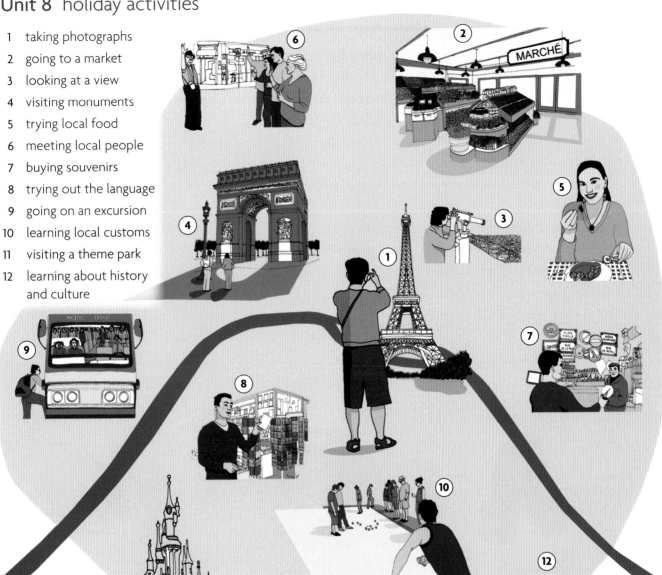

Unit 10 adjectives to talk about the weather

1. bright sunshine
2. dark clouds
3. heavy rain
4. a light shower
5. a strong wind
6. a gentle breeze
7. thick fog
8. a thin mist
9. heavy snow
10. a violent storm

Unit 11 multi-word verbs (2) (with *go* and *put*)

1   put (a fire) out = stop a fire burning
    It was a very bad fire – the firemen only **put** it **out** after six hours.

2   put (someone) up = give them a place to stay or sleep
    We're coming to London next week – can you **put** us **up** in your flat for a few days?

3   put (something) off = change something to a later date
    It was raining very badly, so we **put** the football match **off** until next week.

4   put away = tidy
    This room's a mess – can you **put** everything **away**, please?

5   go up = increase
    The price of food **has gone up** a lot recently.

6   go down = decrease
    My school grades **went down** this year – last year I got a B, this year I got a C.

7   go off = explode
    The bomb **went off** at midnight.

8   go off = ring
    My alarm clock **didn't go off** this morning.

Unit 12 feelings and actions

1   When I'm bored (or tired!), I start to **yawn**.

2   When she's bored, she starts to **daydream**.

3   When they're excited, the kids **jump up and down** and **clap their hands**.

4   When I'm frightened, I **close my eyes**.

5   Some people **scream** when they're frightened.

6   He's very confused – look, he's **scratching his head**.

7   She's very nervous – she's **biting her nails**.

8   When I get nervous, I start to **walk up and down** the room.

9   I think he's angry – he's gone **red in the face**.

10 When he's worried, he often **rubs his forehead**.

Unit 13 personality adjectives

1 He doesn't get angry or upset about things – he's very **easy-going**.
2 She gets angry all the time – she's really **bad-tempered**.
3 She always thinks about what other people want – she's really **thoughtful**.
4 He never thinks about what other people want – he's really **thoughtless**.
5 She listens when you've got problems or bad news – she's very **sympathetic**.
6 He doesn't care if you've had bad news – he's very **unsympathetic**.
7 He never talks about how good he is at things – he's very **modest**.
8 She always talks about how she's the best – she's really **arrogant**.
9 It isn't very easy for him to talk to other people – he's a bit **shy**.
10 She makes new friends very easily – she's very **outgoing**.

Unit 14 verb and noun pairs

1 to make a mess

2 to make an effort

3 to do (the) housework

4 to do your best

5 to have an argument

6 to have an accident

7 to take a break

8 to take an exam

9 to give a talk/presentation/ speech

10 to give (someone) a hand

11 to tell the time

It's true – honestly!

12 to tell the truth

Get it right!

Unit 1

Present simple

We add *s* to the infinitive with *he*, *she* and *it*.
He works in a bank. **Not** *He work in a bank.*
Have and *be* are irregular.
I am, you are, he/she/it is, we are, they are;
I have, you have, he/she/it has, we have, they have

Circle the correct verb.

1 There is / are a cat in the garden.
2 She wears / wear a uniform for school.
3 The boys has / have football practice every Tuesday.
4 Everybody thinks / think it's a good film.

Unit 2

Present simple vs. present continuous

We use the present continuous for something that is happening *now*.
It's raining. **Not** *It rains.*
We use the present simple for an action that happens *regularly*.
It snows every Christmas. **Not** *It's snowing every Christmas.*

a Underline four more mistakes in the text.

Maria is from Rome but she <u>is going</u> to London every summer to stay with her aunt and uncle. Her aunt is being English and her uncle is Italian. She studies at a language school this summer. Today she visits the British Museum for a school project and then she meets a friend from the school to show him the sights of London.

b Correct the spelling of these continuous forms.

1 writting *writing*
2 studing ....
3 seing ....
4 swiming ....
5 comming ....
6 enjoing ....
7 planing ....
8 travveling ....
9 seling ....
10 rainning ....

Unit 4

Past time expressions

We don't usually use *the* with days or months in expressions with *last*.
Last week I went to the doctor.
Not *The last week I went to the doctor.*
Time expressions go at the beginning or at the end of the sentence.
I bought some great jeans **yesterday**.
Not *I bought* **yesterday** *some great jeans.*

Underline the correct sentence.

1 a I went to a wedding the last weekend.
  b <u>I went to a wedding last weekend.</u>
2 a I passed my exam last Friday.
  b I passed my exam the last Friday.
3 a I bought a present for you yesterday.
  b I bought yesterday a present for you.
4 a I visited a week ago my cousins.
  b I visited my cousins a week ago.

Unit 6

Countable and uncountable nouns

There are some nouns we can count. We call them *countable* nouns.
One book, two bananas, etc.
There are some nouns we *can't* count. We call them *uncountable* nouns. These nouns have no plural.
pasta, fruit, etc.

Complete the table with the words in the box.

egg homework bottle music
advice sausage pen information
news shorts cat T-shirt

Countable	Uncountable
egg	....
....	....
....	....

Unit 6

a/an, some and any

We use *a/an* with singular countable nouns (but *an apple* **not** *a apple*).

The school has nice classrooms. **Not** *The school has a nice classrooms.*

We use *some* in positive sentences.

*There are **some** books.* **Not** *There are books.*

*There is **some** wine.* **Not** *There is wine.*

We use *any* in negative sentences or questions.

*There aren't **any** books.* **Not** *There aren't **some** books.*

*Is there **any** water?* **Not** *Is there water?*

Complete the text with the correct form of some of the words in the exercise on countable and uncountable nouns.

Last Thursday, Jake got home from school and listened to some [1] _music_ on the radio for a while. He didn't have any [2] _____ and so he decided to go running with his friend, Miriam. Jake put on some [3] _____ and met Miriam in the park. They ran for an hour and then went home. When he got home, Jake watched the [4] _____ on television and then helped his dad make the dinner. Jake found some [5] _____ and some [6] _____ in the fridge. They made a sausage omelette and opened a [7] _____ of coke. What a perfect dinner!

Unit 6

much and many

We use *much* with uncountable nouns.

Much water **Not** *many water*

We use *many* with plural countable nouns.

Many drinks **Not** *much drinks*

Complete the sentences with *much* or *many*.

1 I'd like to see as _many_ places as you can show me.

2 I didn't see _____ people in town last night.

3 We didn't spend _____ time together last term.

4 My new mobile phone's fantastic! It's got so _____ functions!

5 I love Spain because there are so _____ beautiful places to visit.

Unit 8

Present continuous for future arrangements

We often use the present continuous to talk about plans for the future.

*We're **meeting** in the bar after school.* **Not** *We'll **meet** in the bar after school.*

Complete Naomi's email with the present continuous form of the verbs in brackets.

| from: | Naomi@mailbox.co.uk |
| subject: | Hello! |

Hi Katie!

How are you? It's the last day of school today and then the holidays start – I can't wait!

My cousin [2] _'s coming_ (come) to visit us from Belgium. She [2] _____ (arrive) here at midday tomorrow and we [3] _____ (stay) in Liverpool for the night to see the Leona Lewis concert. I can't believe we've got tickets!

Next week we [4] _____ (go) camping at the seaside. Mum and Dad [5] _____ (drive) us there but then they [6] _____ (return) home – four days at the seaside without Mum and Dad – so cool! There's an adventure centre at the campsite so we [7] _____ (go) canoeing, windsurfing and snorkelling the other three days.

I'll send you a postcard!

Love Naomi

Unit 9

will/won't

We use *will/won't* + *infinitive* to talk about the future.

*We'll **arrive** at 12.00.* **Not** *We'll **arrived** at 12.00.*

[a] Complete the dialogue between Louisa and Sophie. Put the verbs in brackets in the correct tense.

Louisa: I'm so nervous about that exam tomorrow. I'm sure I [1] _'ll fail_ (fail) and Mr Saunders [2] _____ (be) mad at me.

Sophie: Calm down! You ³ _____ (pass) easily, as always. You know you do really well in everything.

Louisa: But Maths is my worst subject. I'm sure I ⁴ _____ (look) at the exam and I ⁵ _____ (no/remember) anything!

Sophie: Come on Louisa, you ⁶ _____ (be) fine!

Louisa: I don't know. I feel so nervous that I'm sure I ⁷ _____ (no/sleep) tonight. Maybe I ⁸ _____ (stay) at home tomorrow.

Sophie: You can't do that Louisa! Mr Saunders ⁹ _____ (give) you the exam the next day. It probably ¹⁰ _____ (no/be) as difficult as you think.

Louisa: OK, thanks Sophie. Maybe I ¹¹ _____ (no/stay) off school after all.

b Complete the sentences about you.

1 Next year I'll _____
_____

2 I think I'll _____
_____ when I leave school.

3 I'll probably _____
_____ when I'm 20.

4 Maybe I'll _____
_____ some time in the future.

Unit 10

too + adjective

We use *too* with adjectives to mean *more than necessary*.

*This bag is **too** heavy.* **Not** *This bag is **very** heavy.*

(Circle) the correct word.

1 He won the championship because he's (very) / too good at tennis.

2 It's 34 °C! That's very / too hot to go out.

3 She sings very / too well. She'll have the most important part in the summer show.

4 There was very / too much pasta for me.

5 I've only got £200 and it costs £300. It's very / too expensive for me to buy.

Unit 10

Adverbs

We use adverbs to describe verbs.

*He swims **slowly**.* **Not** *He swims **slow**.*

Correct the mistakes in these sentences. Look out for spelling mistakes too!

1 I'm <u>realy</u> happy to be here today.   *really*

2 He plays the guitar so good that he was invited to join a band.

3 I normaly wear jeans and a T-shirt in the summer.

4 I have to be carefully when I'm in the car – I'm not a very good driver.

5 My dad finaly bought me a new MP3 player.

Unit 11

must/mustn't and don't have to

Remember *must* and *have to* are similar but *mustn't* and *don't have to* are not!

*You **mustn't** smoke, it's bad for you.* **Not** *You **don't have to** smoke, it's bad for you.*

Natalie is an Olympic swimmer. Write sentences about what she *mustn't do* and what she *doesn't have to do*.

1 smoke
She mustn't smoke.

2 study Latin every day
_____

3 eat unhealthy food
_____

4 go to bed very late
_____

5 lose all her competitions
_____

Unit 12

Adjectives of feeling

We use *-ed* adjectives to describe how someone feels.

*This film is too long and I'm really **bored**.*

We use *-ing* adjectives to describe the thing, place, person or situation that causes that feeling.

*This film's really **boring** because it's too long.*

Complete the sentences with the adjectives in the box.

> frightening   interested   annoying
> annoyed   confusing

1 The film was so __frightening__ I didn't open my eyes.
2 She's _____ in computers, mobile phones and all technology.
3 I'm really _____ because I missed the bus and was late for class.
4 It's a _____ book. There are too many characters and the story's very complicated.
5 He's got lots of _____ habits – like leaving the milk on the table and not in the fridge!

Unit 14

Verb and noun pairs
Before you can use the present perfect you need to know all those irregular past participles!

Put the letters in the correct order to make the past participles then add the infinitive and simple past forms.

infinitive	past participle	simple past
1 _write_	tnweirt _written_	_wrote_
2 _____	koepsn _____	_____
3 _____	teena _____	_____
4 _____	maws _____	_____
5 _____	aknet _____	_____

Unit 14

Present perfect or past simple?
We use the present perfect to talk about finished actions that are important now.

I've eaten Chinese food. **Not** *I ate* Chinese food.

and the simple past for actions in the past that have now finished.

I studied Latin when I was at school. **Not** *I have studied* Latin when I was at school.

Underline the correct sentence.

1 a When have you been to New York?
   b <u>When did you go to New York?</u>
2 a I've never been to Africa but I'd love to!
   b I never went to Africa but I'd love to!
3 a My friend John has arrived yesterday morning.
   b My friend John arrived yesterday morning.
4 a She never learnt English when she was at school.
   b She's never learnt English when she was at school.

Unit 14

Present perfect + *ever/never*
We form the present perfect with *have/has* + past participle.

With the present perfect we use *ever* in questions.

*Have you **ever** been to the UK?* **Not** *Have you **never** been to the UK?*

We use *never* (without *not*) in negative sentences.

*I've **never** been to the UK.* **Not** *I haven't **never** been to the UK.*

Katia's doing a project about her classmates. Write the questions and then answer them about you.

1 Have an accident
   Have you ever had an accident?
   You: _Yes I have. I broke my arm two years ago._
2 lose something important
   _____ ?
   You: _____
3 find something expensive
   _____ ?
   You: _____
4 fall in love
   _____ ?
   You: _____
5 receive a really good present
   _____ ?
   You: _____

Project 1

A presentation about a well-known sports person

1 Brainstorm

a Look through Units 1–4 to find texts that give information about people. Quickly read through these texts again.

b Think of a sportsperson you want to find out about. Think about:

- recent sports events you have seen on TV or read about.
- a person taking part in one of those events who impressed you.
- why this person impressed you.

c Work in a group and ask one student to take notes. Brainstorm ideas to decide who you will do your project on. What do you know about this person and what do you want to find out?

2 Research

With a partner or on your own, find out as much as possible about the person you are working on. Use the internet or look up information in books or magazines, in a library or at home.

Questions to think about:

- When was he/she born?
- What can you find out about his/her childhood?
- What sport does he/she do?
- What was his/her biggest success?
- Why was/is this person so successful?
- What kind of person is he/she?

3 Presentation

In your group, put together all the information you have. Decide how you will organise your presentation. For example:

- Start with a picture that you uncover piece by piece. Ask the class to guess who your presentation is going to be about.
- Take it in turns to present the facts about the person.
- Finish your presentation with each member of the group saying what they admire most about the person.

Project 2
A class survey

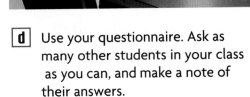

1 Prepare the survey

a Work in small groups (three or four students). Choose one of the following topics:

- Pocket money
- Learning languages
- Going on holiday

b In your group, think of five questions that you can ask other students about your topic, for example:

> **Learning languages**
>
> How often do you get an opportunity to talk to someone in a foreign language?
>
> What do you like / not like about learning a foreign language?
>
> Would you like to learn more languages when you finish school?

c Make a questionnaire with your questions, like this:

> 1 How often do you talk or write to someone in a foreign language?
>
> never / on holiday / once a month / more than once a month
>
> 2 Would you like to learn more languages when you finish school?   Yes/No
>
> 3 What do you like about learning a foreign language?
>
> It's great to communicate with others in another language. ☐
>
> It helps you to understand another culture better. ☐
>
> It's interesting to learn new words. ☐
>
> It's great to understand songs in another language. ☐

Make sure that everyone in your group has a copy of the questionnaire.

d Use your questionnaire. Ask as many other students in your class as you can, and make a note of their answers.

2 Write up the results

a Go back to your group and put all your answers together. For some questions, you can draw a chart.

How often do you talk to someone in a foreign language?

Would you like to learn more languages when you finish school?

b Write a short report about the interviews.

c Arrange your sentences and charts on poster paper, under your topic heading. Add pictures if you want to.

3 Present your information

Use your poster to make a group presentation to the rest of the class.

Project 3
A poster about the future

1 Brainstorm

a You are going to make a poster and give a presentation about life in the future. Work in a group of four or five. In your group, decide on a topic that you all want to work on. For example:

- homes
- towns and cities
- transport
- schools
- clothes
- food
- communication
- weather
- something else

b In your group, decide how far into the future you want to look. Will you talk about the year 2025? 2100? 3000 ...?

c Think about what life will be like in the year you chose. For example, if you chose the topic, food, you can think about these questions:

- Will people eat healthy food?
- Where will their food come from?
- Will they eat more take-away meals?
- Do you think the food will be good to eat?
- Will it be more expensive?
- Will there be enough food for everybody?

Brainstorm ideas and make notes.

2 Make the poster

a Find or draw some pictures that fit with your ideas on the topic. For example, you can find photos from science fiction films in magazines or on the internet, or you can draw your own pictures.

b Write short texts for each of the pictures you are going to use. For example:

In the year 2050, people will live in houses at the bottom of the sea.

c At the top of your project paper, write the title of your presentation. For example:

Homes in the year 2050

Arrange your pictures and short texts on the paper, but leave space at the bottom.

d At the bottom of the poster, write a longer text together. Say what you think about the future you are predicting. For example:

There will be different kinds of homes from the houses we live in now. There will also be houses on the moon and on other planets. People will live in peace and they will live much longer. An old person will be 800 or 900 years old. People will only work for three or four hours a week.

3 Presentation

Present your poster to the other students in your class. Be ready to answer questions about it.

Project 4
A talk on an event that happened this year

1 Listen

CD2 T47 Listen to the beginning of three talks about memorable events that happened this year. What were the events?

2 Choose a topic

Spend some time thinking about the event that you will choose. Will you talk about an event that happened to you or an event that happened somewhere else in the world? Will you talk about something sad, something happy or something funny?

3 Plan

a Think about these questions:
- When and where did the event take place?
- Is there any background information that you will need to explain the event?
- What happened, exactly?
- Why was it memorable? How did you feel about it at the time? How do you feel about it now?

b Make a list of important words you will want to use. If you aren't sure of some words, look them up in a dictionary or ask your teacher. Then use the words to help you make notes for your talk. Don't write everything down in complete sentences – just write important phrases that will help you to remember what you want to say.

c Collect any information you need about your topic. If you can, collect pictures, drawings or photographs that might help you to make your talk more interesting.

d Practise your talk quietly to yourself.

4 Give the talk

Work in a group of four or five. Each student gives his/her talk to the others in the group. Be prepared to answer questions at the end of your talk.

Speaking exercises: Student B

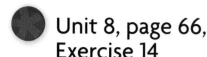

Unit 8, page 66, Exercise 14

Student B: Ask Student A questions about their holiday to find out where they are going, how they are travelling and what kinds of activities they are going to do there.

Student B:

Destination: Tanzania

Dates: 4 January – 25 January

Travel Arrangements: Fly from London Heathrow to Julius Nyerere International Airport, Dar Es Salaam

Hotel: Holiday Inn, Dar Es Salaam

Trips: safari in the Serengeti, trip to Zanzibar

Activities: diving near Oyster Bay

Unit 10, page 80, Exercise 13

Student B: Look at your card. Answer Student A's questions. Then ask Student A questions in order to complete the information on the card.

Famous sportswoman
Full name:
Date of birth:
Place of birth:
Sport:
First team:
In 2004
In 2004, she also
In 2006 and 2007, she

Famous sportsman	
Full name: Kevin Maurice Garnett	
Date of birth: 19 May, 1976	
Place of birth: Mauldin, South Carolina	
Sport: basketball	

Began playing when he was still in primary school

In 1995, he started playing for the Minnesota Timberwolves

In 1999, he became a superstar.

In 2008, he won the NBA championship with the Boston Celtics

Unit 12, page 89, Exercise 3

Student B: Look at the questions. Ask your questions and answer you partner's.

Student B

1 What will you do if you stay at home this weekend?

2 What will you study if you go to university?

3 What will you buy if you go shopping this weekend?

4 How will you feel if your parents ask you to do a lot of housework this evening?

5 Where will you travel if you go abroad on holiday this year?

6 Where will you go if you meet your friends tonight?

Unit 13, page 97, Exercise 3

Student B: Read the role card. Take it in turns to listen to your partner's problem and give advice with *should* or *shouldn't*.

Student B

You love football and you love your favourite football team. But you have a problem. You are going to your best friend's birthday party on Saturday. But now you know that your team has an important match on Saturday, too. You want to see your match, but you don't want to hurt your friend. Should you go to the match? Should you go to the party? Ask Student A.

Irregular verbs

Irregular verbs

Base form	Past simple	Past participle
be	was/were	been
beat	beat	beaten
become	became	become
begin	began	begun
bite	bit	bitten
break	broke	broken
build	built	built
buy	bought	bought
can	could	could
catch	caught	caught
choose	chose	chosen
come	came	come
cut	cut	cut
do	did	done
drive	drove	driven
eat	ate	eaten
fall	fell	fallen
feel	felt	felt
find	found	found
fly	flew	flown
get	got	got
give	gave	given
go	went	gone
grow	grew	grown
have	had	had
hear	heard	heard
hit	hit	hit
hurt	hurt	hurt
keep	kept	kept
know	knew	known
leave	left	left
lose	lost	lost
make	made	made
meet	met	met
put	put	put
read	read	read
ride	rode	ridden
run	ran	run
say	said	said
see	saw	seen
sell	sold	sold
send	sent	sent
sit	sat	sat
sleep	slept	slept
speak	spoke	spoken
stand	stood	stood
swim	swam	swum
take	took	taken
teach	taught	taught
tell	told	told
think	thought	thought
throw	threw	thrown
understand	understood	understood
wake	woke	woken
win	won	won
write	wrote	written

Phonetic symbols

Consonants

/p/	pen
/b/	be
/t/	two
/d/	do
/k/	can
/g/	good
/f/	five
/v/	very
/m/	make
/n/	nice
/ŋ/	sing
/s/	see
/z/	trousers
/w/	we
/l/	listen
/r/	right
/j/	you
/h/	he
/θ/	thing
/ð/	this
/ʃ/	she
/tʃ/	cheese
/ʒ/	usually
/dʒ/	German

Vowels

/æ/	man
/ɑː/	father
/e/	ten
/ɜː/	thirteen
/ə/	mother
/ɪ/	sit
/iː/	see
/ʊ/	book
/uː/	food
/ʌ/	up
/ɒ/	hot
/ɔː/	four

Diphthongs

/eɪ/	great
/aɪ/	fine
/ɔɪ/	boy
/ɪə/	hear
/eə/	chair
/aʊ/	town
/əʊ/	go
/ʊə/	pure

Thanks and acknowledgements

The authors would like to thank a number of people whose support has proved invaluable during the planning, writing and production process of the second edition of *English in Mind*:

The numerous teachers and students in many countries of the world who have used the first edition of *English in Mind*. Their enthusiasm for the course, and the detailed feedback and valuable suggestions we got from many of them, have been an important source of inspiration and guidance for us in the development and creation of the second edition. We would also like to thank those teachers who gave up their valuable time for interviews and focus groups.

Our editorial and production team for their cooperative spirit, their many excellent suggestions and their dedication, which have been characteristic of the entire editorial process: Stephanie Collins, Charlotte Aldis, Hannah Thacker, Flavia Lamborghini, Sophie Clarke, Michael Stubblefield, Angela Page, Laura Clyde, Helen Kenyon, Michelle Simpson and last but not least, James Dingle.

David Crystal for the interview in Unit 7, and to Jon Turner for giving us the idea of using the story of Ulises de la Cruz in Unit 13.

The team at Pentacorbig for giving the book its design; Anne Rosenfeld for the audio recordings; Caroline Jeffries and Sophie Finston at Lightning Pictures for the DVD; Eoin Higgins, Annie Cornford, Lucy Mordini, for their excellent editorial support; and all the other people involved in this course.

The teams of educational consultants, representatives and managers working for Cambridge University Press in various countries around the world.

The leadership team at Cambridge University Press for the spirit of innovation that they have managed to instil in the Press, and for a constructive dialogue over the years: Ron Ragsdale, David Harrison, Hanri Pieterse and Stephen Bourne.

Last but not least, we would like to thank our partners, Mares and Adriana, for their support.

The authors and publishers acknowledge the following sources of copyright material and are grateful for the permissions granted. While every effort has been made, it has not always been possible to identify the sources of all the material used, or to trace all copyright holders. If any omissions are brought to our notice, we will be happy to include the appropriate acknowledgements on reprinting:

You've got a friend in me on p. 35. Words and music by Randy Newman. Copyright © Walt Disney Music (USA) Co (ASCAP). All rights administered by Artemis Muziekuitgeverij BV. All Rights Reserved. Sound a-like recording by Marathon Media International. Copyright © Marathon Media International; When I'm sixty-four on p. 71. Lyrics by John Lennon/Paul McCartney. Copyright © 1967 Sony/ATV Tunes LLC. Administered Sony/ATV Music Publishing. All rights reserved. Used by permission. Sound a-like recording by Marathon Media International. Copyright © Marathon Media International; Wonderful World, Beautiful People on p. 87. Words and music by Jimmy Cliff. Copyright © 1969 Universal/Island Music. Used by permission of Music Sales Limited. All rights for the United States and Canada Administered by Universal – Songs of Polygram International, Inc. All Rights Reserved. Used by permission. Bell Voice Recordings for the sound a-like recording; For the adapted article on p. 88 'Subway hero' from 'Man is rescued by stranger in subway tracks' from The New York Times 3 January 2007. The New York Times. All rights reserved. Used by permission and protected by the Copyright Laws of the United States. The printing, copying, redistribution, or retransmission of the Material without express written permission is prohibited; For the adapted article on pp. 101-103 'Heroic Ulises on a journey of hope' by Sarah Sturdey, The Telegraph 15 February 2007. Copyright © Telegraph Media Group Limited 2007; For the featured Guinness World Records on p. 102. The featured records have been supplied courtesy of Guinness World Records Limited.

The publishers are grateful to the following for permission to reproduce copyright photographs and material:

Key: l = left, c = centre, r = right, t = top, b = bottom, u = upper, lo = lower, f = far

Alamy/©Art Kowalsky p 60 (bl), /©Associated Sports Photography p 100 (tr), /©Mary Evans Picture Library p 72 (palm), /©Manfred Grebler p 108 (tr), /ImagesEurope p 30 (tl), /©David Lyons p 42 (G), /©Photos 12 p 38, /©Kumar Sriskandan p 17 (br), /©Jochen Tack p 42 (L), /©Hugh Threlfall p 45, /©travelib europe p 16 (tr), /©WorldFoto p 40 (tl), /©David Young-Wolff p 44 (tl); ©Biblioteca Universitaria di Bologna p 54 (t); Aquarius Collection/Columbia TriStar p 26 (br); Cache Agency/©Chuck Krall p 86 (l); China Pictorial Supplement, Courtesy of the ITTF; Corbis p 42 (A, J), /©Peter Beck p 91 (tl), /©Bettmann p 69 (cl), /©Kevin Dodge p 55 (l), /©Michel Gounot/Godong p 60 (tr), /©John Harper p 108 (New York), /©Jason Hawkes p 30 (ct), /©Steve Hix/Somos Images p 42 (B), /©Rainer Jensen/dpa p 91 (br), /©Michael A. Keller p 24 (l), /©James Marshall p 46, /©Jacques Pavlovsky/Sygma p 86 (r), /©Anna Peisl p 44 (br), /©Qi Heng/Xinhua Press p 126, /©Reuters pp 62 (b), 104, /©Kelly Redinger/Design Pics p 58 (t), /©Andersen Ross/Blend Images p 55 (r), /©Bjorn Sigurdson/epa p 40 (tr), /©Carlos Silva/Reuters p 29 (tr), /©Zave Smith p 42 (H), /©Pauline St. Denis p 24 (r), /©Thinkstock p 60 (br); © David Crystal p 56 (t); Education Photos/John Walmsley p 42 (D, F); Getty Images/AFP p 82 (b), /AFP/Gent Shkullaku p 102 (bl), /Philip Brown p 43 (t), /Dorling Kindersley/Alex Robinson p 29 (bl), /Hulton Archive p 69 (tl), /Hulton Archive/Archive Holdings Inc. p 69 (tcl), /Hulton Collection p 69 (b), /Sean Justice p 125, /Clive Mason p 43 (b), /David McNew p 26 (tr, br), /National Archives p 30 (cr), /Michael Ochs Archives p 69 (tr), /Photographer's Choice/Luis Veiga p 31 (bl), /Photonica/Colin Gray p 58 (br), /Stock4B/Arne Pastoor p 18 (tr), /Matthew Stockman p 40 (bl), /Stone/David Ball p 30 (br), /Stone/Christopher Bissell p 17 (tr), /Stone/Michael Heinsen p 42 (E), /Stone/Ryan McVay p 108 (concert), /Stone/Adrian Neal p 72 (star signs), /Stone/Les Wies p 72 (bl), /Taxi/Michael Blann p 44 (bl), /Taxi/Frank Herholdt p 59, /Taxi/Jeff Sherman p 91 (tr), /WireImage/Jeff Vespa p 40 (br); ©GUINNESS WORLD RECORDS p 102 (tl, tr); ©Masterfile p 42 (I); Photolibrary.com/age fotostock/EA.Janes p 12 (br), /age fotostock/Javier Larrea p 42 (K), /age fotostock/Jack Milchanowski p 108 (snake), /First Light Associated Photographers/Simon Gardner p 12 (tr), /Fresh Food Images/Dominic Dibbs p 52 (b), /Fresh Food Images/Rob Greig/Time Out p 52 (tr), /Robert Harding Travel/Sergio Pitamitz p 30 (tr), /Japan Travel Bureau/JTB Photo pp 62 (t), 100 (l), /View Pictures/Grant Smith p 52 (tl), /WaterFrame - Underwater Images/Reinhard Dirscherl p 60 (tl), /Josh Westrich p 72 (br); Press Association Images/AP p 75, /AP/Frank Franklin II p 88, /AP/Dolores Ochoa R. p 101, /AP/Seth Wenig p 82 (t), /John Stillwell/PA Archive p 102 (br); Rex Features/Giuliano Bevilacqua p 43 (c), /Everett Collection p 69 (c), /Laurence Kiely p 69 (tcr), /Shout p 44 (tr), /Sipa Press p 80, /The Travel Library p 60 (cr); Shutterstock Images p 91 (c), /Uwe Bumann p 17 (cl), /Els Jooren p 108 (paraglider), /Andrei Merkulov p 42 (C), /Matsonashvili Mikhail p 108 (Maldives), /Maxim Petrichuk p 108 (helicopter), /photogl p 108 (mountain top), /Cora Reed p 72 (background), /RTimages p 108 (trophy), /Sherrianne Talon p 102 (bc), /Ljupco Smokovski p 91 (bl), /Florin Tirlea p 12 (tl), /Zuzule p 108 (horse); Still Pictures/© Ron Giling p 18; The Thayer Collection p 31 (tr).(())

The publishers are grateful to the following illustrators:

Ifan Bates (NB Illustration), Lauren Bishop, Mark Duffin, Kel Dyson (Bright), Dylan Gibson, F&L Productions, Jo Hayman (Eastwing), Clementine Hope (NB Illustration), Graham Kennedy, Paul McCaffrey (Sylvie Poggio), Laura Martinez (Sylvie Poggio), Jonny Mendelsson (Eastwing), Claire Rollet (Illustration), Andrew Selby (Illustration), Mark Watkinson (Illustration), Richard Williams (Eastwing), Ned Woodman (Bright).

The publishers are grateful to the following contributors:

pentacor plc: text design, layouts and cover design

Hilary Fletcher: photo research

Anne Rosenfeld and Dave Morritt: audio recordings

Clare Tonks: Get it Right section

Kerry Maxwell: Corpus research

Commissioned photography (photo stories and cover): Alex Medeville